PLAYING
TALL

Bill Heller

Bonus Books, Inc., Chicago

99   98   97   96   95   5   4   3   2   1

Library of Congress Cataloging-in-Publication Data

Heller, Bill.
Playing tall : the 10 shortest players in NBA history / Bill Heller.
      p.   cm.
   Includes index.
   ISBN 1-56625-045-5 (paper)
   1. Basketball players—United States—Biography.   2. National Basketball
Association.   I. Title.
GV884.A1H38   1995
796.323'092'2—dc20
[B]   95-19367

Bonus Books, Inc.
160 East Illinois Street
Chicago, Illinois 60611

*Cover photos: Background photo (Spud Webb) courtesy of the Atlanta Hawks.
Foreground photo (Monte Towe) courtesy of Ken Hill, Sports Hotline, and
Frances Towe.*

Printed in the United States of America

To my cousin Wendy

Other books by Bill Heller:

Harness Overlays: Beat the Favorite
Obsession: Bill Musselman's Relentless Request
Overlay, Overlay: How to Bet Horses Like a Pro
Travelin' Sam, America's Sports Ambassador *
The Will to Win: The Ron Turcotte Story *

* Not published by Bonus Books.

Table of Contents

Acknowledgements

An incredible number of people helped with the writing and research for *Playing Tall*. For many, it meant interrupting an already hectic schedule in the NBA. They did so graciously.

Indiana Pacers Coach Larry Brown somehow found time in the middle of the 1994-95 season to write the foreword. Thanks, coach. Thanks, too, to David Benner and Mary Kay Hruskocy of the Pacers' Media Relations.

Bill Himmelman, the NBA Historian, was an invaluable help in contacting the players profiled here. He literally saved the author months of work.

The entire NBA Media Relations Office was an immense help, especially Evan Silverman and my friend, Chris Ekstrand.

Keith Jennings of Golden State could not have been more helpful. Thanks, too, to his parents, Ken and Zerlene, and Keith's brother Kirk. Former Warriors Coach Don Nelson and Assistant Coach Donn Nelson donated their time. Golden State's Director of Media Relations Julie Marvel and her staff went the extra mile to help several times. North Carolina State Head Coach Les Robinson, who coached Keith at East Tennessee State, was a valued interview. East Tennessee State Sports Information Director Lyn Mitchell and her staff provided important material.

Greg Grant did a series of phone interviews, which were supplemented wonderfully by a video and interview provided by Rider Coach Kevin Bannon, Greg's former coach at

Trenton State. Thanks to Alex Martins and Lori Hamamoto of the Orlando Magic Media Relations. Thanks to Ann Bready, Trenton State's Sports Information Director.

Ralph "Buckshot" O'Brien was kind enough to do several interviews. He also put together a carton of scrapbooks and old articles which were extremely helpful. Thanks to Jim McGrath, Butler University's Sports Information Director for college clips about Buckshot.

Monte Towe found time in his coaching schedule for several interviews. Monte's mom, Frances, provided several articles and photos, as well as a fascinating interview. Ken Hill, editor and writer of the *Sports Hotline*, has covered Monte all during his athletic career and furnished several of his excellent articles. Thanks to Monte's former coach at North Carolina State, Norm Sloan, and to Monte's former college and pro teammate, David Thompson. North Carolina State's Sports Information Office, Mark Bockelman, Joan von Thron, Caffie Darder and Carter Cheves, who do an outstanding media guide, were a big help for both Monte and Spud Webb, who also played at NC State.

Hershey Carl did several interviews and furnished valuable articles and photos. Many thanks to DePaul coaching legend Ray Meyer. Thanks to Hershey's good friend Ira Berkow of *The New York Times* for sharing his work and opinions, to Hershey's brother, Sam, and to Norm Sonju, General Manager of the Dallas Mavericks. Also thanks to DePaul Sports Information Director John Lanctot.

Calvin Murphy interrupted his TV schedule to do a set of interviews. A gigantic thank you to Rose Pietrzak and Zina Miller of the Houston Rockets Media Relations, as well as to Calvin's brother, Bob Miller. Calvin's former high school coach Jack Cronin did a helpful interview. "Taps, The Gentleman Coach," a book about Niagara University Coach Taps Gallagher written by a late friend of the author, Lloyd Paterson, had much helpful material. Utah Jazz President and former Head Coach Frank Layden, who was Calvin's coach at Niagara, provided his usual dynamic interview. Thanks to Jim Mauro and Lisa Sparks of Niagara's Sports Information.

Muggsy Bogues gave up a free Sunday afternoon for an interview. Thanks to Charlotte Coach Allan Bristow, TV analyst Mike Gminski and Harold Kaufman and Jason Brennan of the Hornets' Media Relations. Thanks to John Justus and his staff at Wake Forest Sports Information.

Murray Wier did several interviews and sent important articles and photos. Thanks to Gary Hveem, Mike Woodley and Howard Vernon, Jr., for interviews about Murray, and thanks to Eric Capper, the University of Iowa Sports Information Director, and Martha Baker of Waterloo High School.

Charlie Criss endured a bushel of interviews. Thanks to TBS TV analyst Hubie Brown, who coached Charlie with the Atlanta Hawks, for an excellent and insightful interview. Thanks to University of Illinois Coach, Lou Henson, who coached Charlie at New Mexico State, and Tom James, Serena Burrell and the rest of the staff at New Mexico State Sports Information.

Thanks to Spud Webb, Sacramento Coach Garry St. Jean and Travis Stanley of Sacramento Media Relations.

Thanks to Derek Harper, Anthony Mason and Charles Smith of the New York Knicks, Tim Hardaway of Golden State, Orlando Magic Player/Assistant Coach Tree Rollins and NBA Hall of Famer Bob Cousy.

Thanks to John Cirillo, Chris Brienza and Eric Green of the Knicks Media Relations, Arthur Triche, Jon Steinberg and the staff of the Atlanta Hawks Media Relations, and Tommy Sheppard and Mike Behrenhausen of the Denver Nuggets Media Relations.

Thanks to Brett Meister, Director of Public Relations, and Cindy Jordan of the Continental Basketball Association, Gary Johnson and Julie Quickel of the NCAA, Clay Stoldt of Oklahoma City University Sports Information, David Rosenblatt of the Auburn University Archives, and Steve Allen of Purdue University Sports Information.

Personal thanks to Seattle Supersonics Coach George Karl, Harry Downie, Nan Veder, and my proofreaders, Stu and Sue Milstein.

Special thanks to my lifetime editor, my wife Anna, and the brains of our operation, six-year-old Bubba, a.k.a. Benjamin.

Foreword

'm really happy to write the foreword for this book because basketball has given me a unique opportunity without having to worry about size. Not only did I get a chance to play, but I'm also able to do what I love to do more than anything, which is to teach and coach.

I don't think any small player looks at his size as a handicap, at least not the ones that have made it to the professional level. I would think most small players would feel they are special because they have the ability to play the game. When people hear you can't do something, you have a tendency to want to do it and do it well. I believe that's probably what all the players mentioned in this book would say.

As for my playing career, there were a significant number of small players in the old American Basketball Association, and I think that league should certainly receive a lot of credit because it gave small guys the opportunity. You can look around and see.

I also think the three-point shot gave people a reason to play smaller people, but I don't think that should have been the reason. I think little guys were always capable of playing on this level, but nobody ever gave them the chance. When little guys started having success, that made people aware that they could play at the top level. They didn't look at what guys couldn't do and their deficiencies. They started to look at what guys could do and their strengths, which are certainly speed and quickness, and, in a lot of cases, competitiveness, or they wouldn't have made it on that level.

I think if you looked at the rosters of the ABA, there were so many teams with small guys—maybe not under 5-foot-10 but certainly a lot of six feet and under. I think it was because coaches had a different attitude in terms of what a smaller player could do. I think they might have focused on their strengths rather than what they couldn't do.

In the NBA, the idea was that the guards are John Havlicek, Oscar Robertson and Jerry West—how is the little guy going to guard them? Instead of worrying about how the little guard would guard them, which obviously no one was able to do anyway, how were they going to guard the little guy?

I think the ABA approached it that way and gave guys a chance, and when people saw the success the small guys were having in the ABA, it was easier to accept that in the NBA.

— Larry Brown
January 1995

Larry Brown, coach of the Indiana Pacers, is 5-foot-9, although during his ABA days he was often listed in the game program as taller. He was an outstanding collegiate player at the University of North Carolina and was a member of the U.S. Gold Medal Olympic Team in 1964. He played on five different teams in five ABA seasons, averaging 11.2 points and 6.7 assists. He played on an ABA championship team with Oakland in 1968-1969, and holds the ABA record for assists in one game (23). He led the ABA in assists three consecutive years. He was All-ABA Second Team in 1968 and MVP of the All-Star Game that season when he had 17 points, five assists and three rebounds. He also played in two other All-Star Games.

He coached for four seasons in the ABA and was named Coach of the Year in three of them. He later coached the University of Kansas to the 1987-88 NCAA National Championship.

Larry Brown coached the Pacers to their first Central Division title and their best NBA record ever (52-30) in 1994-1995.

The only other ABA player under 5-10 was Jerry Dover, who played four games with Memphis in the 1971-72 season.

Ground Rules

Basketball players have never been noted for accurately disclosing their height—at any level. Six feet sounds a heck of a lot better than 5-11 or even 5-10.

For this book, there was only one source to turn to: *The NBA Encyclopedia*, which was totally revised and updated for the 1994-95 season, and edited by Alex Sachere.

Nearly 2,400 players have competed in the NBA from 1949 through 1995. Ten have been under 5-10. These ten.

CHAPTER
1

A Chance to Play

Y ou're too short."
They've heard it all their lives.

"Every year," Spud Webb said. "I didn't listen to it. If I listened to it, I'd be a season ticket holder somewhere."

At what level should the short player stop trying and just give up, accede to the overwhelming popular opinion? Grade school? High school? College? Pro?

What is it that burns inside an athlete which never gives in and never lets go?

What possessed Charlie Criss to keep chasing his dream until he was 28 years old?

Why didn't Hershey Carl give up when he couldn't get a minute of playing time on the freshman team at the University of Illinois?

What is it that drove Monte Towe to dribble a basketball three-quarters of a mile back and forth from school every day?

How exactly did Calvin Murphy play so obliviously of his height that he's now in the Hall of Fame?

How did Murray Wier and Ralph "Buckshot" O'Brien make it to the NBA in the '50s, and Muggsy Bogues, Spud Webb, Keith "Mister" Jennings and Greg Grant in the '80s and '90s?

Collectively, they are the 10 shortest players in the NBA's 46-year history, the only ones under 5-foot-10 to appear in even a single game. A handful of them had the audacity to build a career.

"This may sound crazy, but I think their size is an advantage," said Frank Layden, President of the Utah Jazz—and Calvin Murphy's former coach at Niagara University. "I think you're better off being 5-7 than being 6-1. If you're 6-1, there's another 6-1 guy to guard you. If you're 5-7, who guards you?

"Who spends the energy to post these guys up? You can't do it because people have been posting them up all their lives. They adjust. Most of them learn to shoot from outside. They learn how to dribble with either hand. They're usually coachable. They're underdogs and they make up for it with mental toughness."

It goes with the territory.

Imagine the nerve it takes 5-foot-3 Muggsy Bogues to excel at point guard for the Charlotte Hornets when he's lined up against Orlando's 6-7 Penny Hardaway or 6-4 Derek Harper of the Knicks or Seattle's 6-4 Gary Payton.

"I think Muggsy does a good job of pushing the basketball with his speed," Harper said. "Defensively, he's a pest because he's right down on the floor and he's able to move in front of you all the time. He creates a lot of problems for you, and I think Muggsy is one of those guys that is getting better and better."

The words are nice. But the bottom line is that Muggsy does succeed, as do his slightly taller contemporaries. Spud Webb, Muggsy and Keith Jennings finished the 1994-95 season ranked first (.934), fifth (.889) and 10th (.876) in the NBA, respectively, in free throw percentage. Muggsy, who averaged a career high 11.1 points, was fifth (8.7) in the league in assists. Spud was 18th (6.2), while averaging 11.6 points.

A slice of the 1994-95 season:

Saturday, February 18—Muggsy makes seven of eight shots from the field—he didn't get any foul shots—for 14 points and 11 assists to lead host Charlotte past Detroit, 110-88.

Monday, February 20—Spud makes 11 of 13 field goal attempts and his lone two foul shots for 24 points, and has eight assists, but the visiting Sacramento Kings lose to the Pistons, 99-93. In Oakland, Keith comes off the bench for 10 points as the Golden State Warriors beat Philadelphia, 98-85.

Wednesday, February 22—Charlotte downs visiting Sacramento, 100-89, as Muggsy goes six of eight from the field and makes all seven foul shots for 19 points and seven assists. Spud makes two of four field goals and his only two foul shots for six points. The Warriors are thrashed 107-89 by visiting Portland, but Keith again has a good game off the bench, 13 points and a team-high six assists.

Every night, these three were making an impact in the NBA.

A point guard's efficiency can be measured by his assist to turnover ratio: the number of baskets he sets up for his teammates compared to the number of times he turns the ball over to the other team. In the '94-95 season, Muggsy was No. 1 (5.11 to 1) in the NBA by a clear margin. Vinnie Del Negro of San Antonio was a distant second (4.04), while Keith was 10th (3.11). It was the sixth time in the last seven years that Muggsy led the NBA in that statistic.

This doesn't suggest that Muggsy is one of the best point guards in the league now—though he may well be—but it certainly shoots to oblivion the notion that an undersized player can't contribute in the NBA.

Even more than the numbers, though, Muggsy helped his Hornets to contend in the Central Division, while Sacramento had its best season since the Dark Ages with Spud leading the way.

The NBA has changed. "It's speeded up," Muggsy said.

Penny Hardaway today—and Magic Johnson before him—shows how effective a tall man can be at point guard. But the NBA of the '90s does have room for players a foot shorter. They just have to be really good.

"In the old days, you had a narrow scope of vision," Spud Webb's coach at Sacramento, Garry St. Jean, said. "You had to have two big guards. The times have changed. Ten to 15 years ago, there were people posting up all the time. Now people are doubling the post quicker and helping out. It's not as big a concern as it was then."

Spud remembers when he first came into the league in 1985, when every point guard was asked to measure up to 6-9 Magic Johnson: "Everybody was looking for another Magic Johnson, but there was only one special one like him."

Some coaches, though, were never so concerned with a short player's liabilities that they didn't also see the other side of the equation. Certainly a taller guard can post up a Muggsy Bogues. But if he does, he's apt to get double-teamed. If he shoots, he's almost certainly in too deep to get back on defense. It's the same scenario if there's a turnover. And who wants Muggsy in their face every single time they bring the ball upcourt? Who can stay with him when he's got the ball?

"Muggsy, he's probably my favorite," Seattle Coach George Karl said. "He just plays with such a passion. He plays what I call the right way. He just enjoys it. He has a good attitude. He has a relationship with his teammates all the time. I think, because of that, he's a really good floor leader."

Five-foot-nine Indiana Pacers Coach Larry Brown, who played in the ABA for five seasons, was aware of the bias against short players but never really understood it, especially when it was directed at him: "When I got drafted out of college by Baltimore (of the NBA), their general manager came to see me. He said, 'Golly, you're smaller than we thought. How are you going to guard Oscar Robertson or Jerry West or Havlicek?'

"My response was that nobody was guarding them. They were averaging 30 to 35 points a game. I don't know if he appreciated that. They didn't invite me to camp.

"I never looked at my size as a disadvantage. I don't think any player would look at it as a disadvantage. You just play the game. I never worried about size limiting me at all."

Yet, it almost seemed taboo for NBA teams to have a player under six feet, let alone under 5-10. From 1963 to 1975, there wasn't a single one. "Nobody wanted to take a chance," Brown said.

He did, using Monte Towe with the Denver Nuggets for a single season in both the ABA and NBA. "He was like having a coach on the floor," Brown said. "He could run a team. He could shoot the ball, and he had great range. He was unselfish. He got to play in the pros because of those skills.

"There's a place for everybody. Little guys have to have some great skills. You can't be small and not quick. You can't be small and not tough and competitive."

These 10 were. They were stubborn and resourceful and so determined that they not only compensated for their size, but also convinced one coach after another that they were a positive addition to their basketball teams.

"It's still a game where speed and quickness separate the men from the boys," 6-foot-1 Hall of Fame point guard Bob Cousy said. "If you're under 5-10, it's a disadvantage, but you can overcome it if you have exceptional skills: speed, quickness and jumping ability. These guys may be 5-3 or 5-7, but they play like they're much taller."

The bottom line is this:

You can measure height. You can't measure heart.

Muggsy
5-3

When Michael Jordan was gone, Muggsy Bogues was the only NBA player I'd pay to see," Utah Jazz President Frank Layden said.

He's got plenty of company.

How could anybody watch 5-foot-3 Tyrone "Muggsy" Bogues, the shortest player in the history of the NBA, perform and not marvel?

"The average Joe out there in the stands can really relate to a guy like Muggsy," former Golden State Assistant Coach Donn Nelson said. "He is actually bigger than him. He ends up pulling for him. Muggsy's a guy that has overcome all odds to just set foot in the League, not to mention have tremendous success."

And, judged in any context possible, be sure that Muggsy Bogues is having tremendous success in the NBA. In

1994-95, he was first in the league in assist to turnover ratio, fifth in assists and fifth in free throw percentage, while averaging a career high 11.1 points and an astounding 3.3 rebounds a game.

He was and is the architect of one of the NBA's best teams, the Charlotte Hornets. With him handling the ball, and superstars Alonzo Mourning and Larry Johnson healthy again, Charlotte posted its best record (50-32) in its seven-year franchise history in 1994-95. The Hornets are, and will be for years, legitimate title contenders with their 5-3 point guard showing the way.

"When you're playing against the Hornets, you always think Larry Johnson or Alonzo is the team leader, but then you find out Muggsy is the heart and soul," Muggsy's former backcourt mate, Hersey Hawkins, said.

Former Charlotte center Mike Gminski, who is now a TV analyst for the Hornets, said, "Muggsy's just got incredible desire and confidence in himself and his own abilities. We all know that he's short, but he's very strong and powerfully built and has great endurance and durability. I think he's lasted because of his strength more than anything. You look at Spud Webb. He's a little more frail than Muggsy but still not less surprising."

Gminski said he still is surprised every time he sees Muggsy play: "Probably more so than any other player I've ever seen."

And, of all people, New York Knicks strongman forward Anthony Mason knows exactly how Muggsy has pulled it off: "His heart is bigger than he is."

It must be to run and play where he does.

"People always say we'll never see another Larry Bird," Charlotte Coach Allan Bristow said. "But I've always felt we have a better chance of seeing another Larry Bird than we do another Muggsy Bogues. Nobody has done what Muggsy is doing."

Through it all, from being told to become a wrestler instead of a basketball player as a youngster, from struggling initially at Wake Forest University, from frustrating NBA seasons in Washington, and in Charlotte, too, until emerging as a legitimate NBA starting point guard, Muggsy has conducted himself with grace. He has been, and likely always will be, comfortable with a public which frequently finds his accomplishments amazing. "I know people respect me and the things I do, not just look at me because of my size," he said.

When opposing NBA point guards, anywhere from four to 16 inches taller than he is, look at Muggsy at the start of the game, they know they will have a challenging evening, to say the least. Yes, they have an obvious height advantage on offense, and they may try to exploit that by posting him up, but they'll earn any points they get because he'll be in their face, or at their knees, every time they try to dribble the ball.

"You got to watch out for those guys, because they get their hands down where you dribble," Golden State's All-Star guard Tim Hardaway said. "Muggsy is quick. But it goes both ways. He's got to come back on the other end and take some of what I'm going to give him. But he is crazy on defense. He's just a pain in the butt."

Boston's Sherman Douglas said of Muggsy, "He's so annoying you want to slap him."

Sacramento's Spud Webb said, "Muggsy is so quick and so low to the ground that you don't know where he is. You try to keep an eye on him and it throws you off."

Doc Rivers of San Antonio knows the feeling: "The toughest part about playing against Muggsy is when he's behind me. I never know where he is. You can see the big guys out of the corner of your eye. But when Muggsy's behind me, there's no telling where he's coming from."

All this makes Muggsy happy. "I'm always trying to get a steal," he said. "I'm always pressuring my opponent, trying to throw him off rhythm. I play each possession like it's the last one of the game."

While Muggsy is relentless on defense, he's unique on offense. There has never been a point guard in the NBA quite like him, not one as quick and creative. "Muggsy just dominates with his quickness," New York Knicks Coach Don Nelson said. "He has a limited range with his shot, but he's such a great creator and passer that he's a dominant force."

In the NBA. Imagine that.

Muggsy isn't even similar to the other short players who preceded him. "I think I am different from the other small guards," he said in an interview with Andy English in the *High Point* (North Carolina) *Enterprise.* "I am not taking anything away from them. My game is different from Spud, Michael Adams or even Calvin Murphy. They have more of a scoring mentality. Me, I'm a creator. I try to find my teammates and take the shot if it is there. I could become more of a scorer, but there is no place on our team for that. We have talent and scorers, and we can win by me being unselfish and doing other things. When you've got finishers such as Larry and Zo [Mourning], you want to get them the ball."

And he does. Others told him that he'd never make it, but he never subscribed to that opinion. "Believe it or not, I never doubted myself," he said. "It may be arrogant, but I always believed. It comes from my mom. It comes from my upbringing. I was a hard-nosed guy who wouldn't take no for an answer. I felt it's very hard for others to believe in you if you don't believe in yourself. I always thought I could play."

Regardless of the obstacles.

Tyrone Curtis Bogues, born January 9, 1965, was the third son and fourth child of 4-foot-11 Elaine and 5-6 Richard Bogues, who worked the docks as a stevedore in Baltimore.

Muggsy in 1984.
Courtesy of Wake Forest University

His mother has always called her son Ty. "He had the cutest little nose and the cutest little cheeks," she said.

In an interview with Charles Chandler of the *Charlotte Observer*, Leon Howard recalled his first impressions of Muggsy at a summer camp. Howard, who played basketball at Johnson

C. Smith University in Charlotte, North Carolina, in the early
'60s, was Director of the Lafayette Court Recreation Center
in Baltimore. Muggsy was five years old when he went there.
And tiny.

"Even then he was the smallest kid around," Howard said.

But Muggsy pleaded with him daily to be the one selected
to hold the American flag when the children recited the
Pledge of Allegiance. "I remember so well him walking out
with the flag in his left hand and his right hand over his
heart," Howard said.

Muggsy began playing organized basketball at a camp there
when he was eight. "You could tell he was going to be a star,"
Howard said. "You watch the way a person walks, like a
peacock, head up with a little strut. That's what he had, head
up with a little strut. He wasn't afraid of anybody.

"You look at him [now] at 5-3. Never in my life, never in
your life, probably never in another 100 years will there be
another kid that good that size. You can almost say it's a
miracle."

There was nothing miraculous about Muggsy's childhood.
He grew up in the Lafayette projects in East Baltimore,
witnessing drugs, crimes and death with frightening regular-
ity. "It was right outside my door—drugs, shooting, people
getting killed," he said.

He saw a man stab another with an ice pick, and a man
beaten to death with a baseball bat. He saw a kid get into an
argument during a basketball game, leave, return with a gun
and shoot the kid he had been arguing with in the back. "It's
tough to be a little kid in the projects," he said.

He'll always have souvenirs. When he was five, he was shot
outside a store after someone else threw a rock through the
store window and the owner came out firing with a shotgun.
In his book, *In The Land Of Giants*, written with David
Levine, Muggsy recounted:

"Shotgun pellets hit me in the right arm, on the inside of
the biceps and all up and down my right leg. Luckily, the

wounds were not serious. They removed as many of the pellets as they could, patched me up and sent me home. They didn't get all the pellets, though, and I still have a few in my arm to this day. They don't hurt or anything, but I can feel them there. They always remind me of how precious life is and how quickly it can be taken away. They remind me of all the friends I've lost. And I know it could as easily have been me as them. You don't have to be a bad guy to die in the streets. Plenty of good people die, too."

That wasn't the only difficult experience he had growing up. He was 12 when his father was sentenced to 20 years in federal prison for armed robbery. His mother, who had left high school in the 11th grade when pregnant with her first child, learned typing, earned a high school equivalency certificate, and got a job as a secretary to support her family.

These were difficult times for Muggsy's family. He found relief every time he stepped on a basketball court, and he did that every chance he could, either on the playgrounds or at the Lafayette Rec Center.

He guesses he was eight when he first was advised that he'd never make it in basketball. "They said I should stick with wrestling where size doesn't matter," he said. "That's what drove me. I love the game, and the game is what I was interested in. I kept hearing it, though I knew I was successful against the players I was facing."

He found a role model in 5-5 Dwayne Wood, who played at famed Dunbar High in Baltimore and then at Virginia State. "Of course I knew about Charlie Criss and Calvin Murphy, but Dwayne hit home," Muggsy said. "He was a couple of years older than myself, and he was in front of my face. I kind of patterned my game after him."

Wood, in return, gave the kid his nickname. Two reasons. He reminded Wood of the Bowery Boys movie character, Muggsy, who was leader of the gang. Also, young Bogues seemed to consistently mug people on defense.

The name fit.

His aspirations didn't. Steadily, he heard the admonition: Give up basketball for another sport. "I can still picture in my mind sitting in the kitchen eating cereal, telling my mom, and her saying, 'Don't believe it. No one can be an expert on your life if they don't know what's inside you,'" Muggsy said.

He showed what was inside on the court.

He dribbled the ball everywhere, up and down stairs, taking out the trash, through a slalom course of cardboard boxes he set up. "As a kid, I always had a ball with me," he said.

At Dunbar, he was part of an incredibly successful program operated by Coach Bob Wade, who later became coach at the University of Maryland. "Coach was like a father to me," Muggsy said. "He's been like that throughout my career." The Poets went 59-0, 28-0 in Muggsy's junior season and 31-0 when he was a senior. The team produced four NBA players: his closest friend, Reggie Williams (now with Denver), David Wingate (with Seattle), Muggsy, and the late Reggie Lewis, another of Muggsy's closest friends who became an NBA star with the Boston Celtics before his untimely death from heart problems in July of 1993.

"We were all stars in our own right," Muggsy said. "We pretty much got equal attention. We had relationships where it didn't matter who got the reputation. Coach kept us from getting egotistical with one another. We had a special program there with Coach Wade."

Constantly, though, Muggsy was reminded of his size, as if one time he would just listen and give up basketball: "What bugged me was that no one ever said to me, 'Muggsy, you shouldn't play because you aren't good enough.' It was always, 'You can't play because you are too short.'"

One of his most legendary high school games was in Muggsy's junior year, when the undefeated Poets, ranked No. 2 in Baltimore behind unbeaten Calvert Hall, traveled to Camden High School, New Jersey, to face the No. 1 team in the nation, featuring future college stars Billy Thompson,

Milt Wagner and point guard Kevin Walls, the trio that would lead the University of Louisville to the 1986 NCAA National Championship.

The Camden players snickered at Muggsy when the starting line-ups were introduced. "I could see the players and the fans laughing and joking," Muggsy said. "Kevin Walls came out, and when he came near me he laughed and pointed at me, and then at himself, as if he was telling the crowd, 'Hey, I got the little one.' He thought I was a joke or something. When he pointed at me, the entire crowd laughed at me."

Muggsy got the last laugh. He held Walls to nine points and stole the ball from him seven times, including three in a row, as Dunbar crushed Camden, 84-59.

Muggsy's senior year began with a 12-point win against powerful DeMatha High of Washington, D.C., led by future Duke star Danny Ferry, now with the Cleveland Cavs. DeMatha Coach Morgan Wooten called Dunbar the best team he'd ever seen: "I've never seen one better. The thing that Dunbar has that none of these other teams had is Muggsy Bogues. Monte Towe was a better outside shooter, but Bogues is better at everything else."

But what college wanted a 5-3 guard? The offers didn't pile up.

Muggsy accepted one from Wake Forest, and it challenged him in ways he never expected. "That was tough," he said. "First time leaving Baltimore. Pretty much a predominately white atmosphere. That's the first time I faced that. It was the first time I had time to myself without people pushing me, without me knowing what I needed to do and how much time I had to do it. The academics were very difficult."

The athletics, too. For the first time in his life, Muggsy was anything but the man with the ball. In his freshman season, he averaged just 1.2 points, 1.7 assists and 9.8 minutes a game, playing in each one but starting in none of them.

Wake Forest made it to the Final Eight of the 1984 NCAA Tournament before losing to Houston's Phi Slamma Jamma, featuring Hakeem (then Akeem) Olajuwon and Clyde Drexler. Wake Forest, which finished 23-9, hung tough with the Cougars, losing 68-63, but Muggsy played just two minutes.

He thought of quitting. But he didn't. "I looked at it as a challenge," he said. "This is where I chose to go. This is what I wanted. It got easier."

In his ensuing three seasons at Wake Forest, he led the Atlantic Coast Conference in assists and minutes played.

Averaging 35.3 minutes a game, he hiked his sophomore numbers up to 7.1 assists, 6.6 points and 2.4 rebounds, but the Demon Deacons slipped to 15-14.

Bob Staak replaced Carl Tacy as head coach at Wake Forest in Muggsy's junior season. Wake slipped to 8-21, but Muggsy averaged 11.3 points and 3.1 rebounds, and ACC highs in assists (8.4) and steals (3.1). He received the Murray Greason Award, named for Wake Forest's winningest coach (288-243), as the team's Most Valuable Player.

After the season, he was one of 50 players invited to the United States National Team Trials for the 1986 World Basketball Championship in Spain that summer. He became the starting point guard for the U.S. Team, which won the World Championship. His teammates included David Robinson, Kenny Smith, Derrick McKey and Steve Kerr—all now in the NBA. In the championship game against the Soviet Union, Muggsy didn't score but had 10 steals and five assists.

Muggsy was dubbed "La Chispa Negra," the black spark. Reporter Pedro Luis Gomez wrote of Muggsy in the local *El Pais* newspaper: "He has nerves of steel and super-flexible muscles, and on the court he appears to be a little brother of his teammates, but it is he who orders, commands and directs."

But as his collegiate career commanded more attention, he grew tired of comparisons to Spud Webb, two years his senior and four inches taller. They played against each other for two seasons when Spud was at North Carolina State, before he

Muggsy flies above NC State.
Courtesy of Wake Forest University

moved on to the NBA. "Even though we had two completely different games, people concentrated just on our size," Muggsy said. "I hated that. I wanted to be covered for my game, not for my height."

He led the Demon Deacons (14-15) in scoring as a senior (14.8), averaged 9.5 assists—Avery Johnson of Southern-Baton Rouge, now with the San Antonio Spurs, led the country at 10.74—and was second among ACC guards in rebounding at 3.8. He set a school and ACC record for career assists and steals, with 781 and 275, respectively. He received the Frances Pomery Naismith Award as the nation's best collegiate player under six feet tall. He was again named team MVP. And his number, 14, was retired.

Muggsy was a hit at Wake Forest and a smash overseas. But that hardly meant he was done proving himself. He had the ridiculous notion that he would succeed at the next level, the NBA level.

He plainly didn't care that nobody even close to his size had ever appeared in a single game. If you're 5-3, 5-7 is a big difference, and only two 5-7 players had made it to the NBA: Monte Towe and Spud. Charlie Criss was 5-8 and Calvin Murphy 5-9. The players before Muggsy's time, Murray Wier, Ralph "Buckshot" O'Brien and Hershey Carl were 5-9, 5-9 and 5-9 1/2, respectively.

Muggsy was trying to make NBA history, and he instantly did when the Washington Bullets made him the 12th selection in the 1987 Draft. He, Reggie Williams (Clippers—No. 4 pick) and Reggie Lewis (Celtics—No. 22 pick) hold the distinction of being three high school teammates all selected in the first round of the NBA Draft. Another teammate, a year older, David Wingate, had been taken in the second round of the 1986 Draft by the Philadelphia 76ers (44th pick overall).

To his credit, Muggsy spent that summer playing with the Rhode Island Gulls of the United States Basketball League, a minor league where he got to play against NBA All-Star

Micheal Ray Richardson and Nancy Lieberman, widely re-garded as the best woman player of her time. "She was competitive," Muggsy said. "She held her own."

Then it was time for the NBA. "It was like a big weight lifted off my shoulder when I arrived in the NBA," Muggsy said. "This is what I wanted. This is what I'd always dreamt, getting on the floor with NBA players, trying to take my game to the next level. It finally happened."

Just about every NBA rookie is stunned by the level of talent he's confronted with in his first training camp. Muggsy was no different, although he had the added disadvantage of even greater height discrepancies. "I played against taller guys pretty much my whole career," he said. "This was just taller players who were talented. But it was tough. I was nervous going into training camp. In college, you might not face a good guard every night. In the pros you do."

One of the first things Muggsy did with his NBA money was buy his mother a four bedroom house in Ellicott City, Maryland. Then he hired an attorney to help his father get out of prison. His father would be paroled, but not until December 21, 1988, when Muggsy was with the Charlotte Hornets.

Charlotte was a city Muggsy would come to love.

With the Bullets, Muggsy averaged 5.0 points and a team-high 5.1 assists in 1987-88. His 404 assists were 143 higher than anyone else on the team. Muggsy started 14 of the 79 games he played in, but he wasn't thrilled to be playing an average of only 20.6 minutes.

But the Bullets weren't thrilled with him either. So they left him off their protected list of eight players in the 1988 Expansion Draft, when the NBA's two newest teams, the Charlotte Hornets and the Miami Heat, would select the first members of their first team. On June 23, 1988, the Hornets made Muggsy their third pick after Dell Curry and center Dave Hoppen. With their fourth pick, Charlotte selected center Mike Brown and immediately traded him to the Utah

Jazz for Kelly Tripucka, who would lead the Hornets in scoring in their first two seasons. Charlotte's ensuing selections were Rickey Green, Michael Holton, Michael Brooks, Bernard Thompson, Ralph Lewis, Clinton Wheeler and Sedric Toney.

From that group—as well as the Hornets' 1988 college draft picks, Rex Chapman, Tom Tolbert and Jeff Moore—two players have been with Charlotte since Day One. They are pictured on the cover of the Hornets' 1994-95 Media Guide: Muggsy for his second Charlotte MVP Award, and his close friend Dell Curry, who won the NBA's 1993-94 Sixth Man Award as the most valuable substitute in the league. "Dell and I were originals," Muggsy said. "We grew with the franchise."

Slowly.

NBA expansion franchises routinely get hammered in their initial season, and Charlotte was a prime example, going 20-62. If that wasn't bad enough for Muggsy, he also had to come to terms with the painful reality that Charlotte Coach Dick Harter didn't think his team could win with Muggsy starting. Muggsy started just 21 of the 79 games he played, averaging 22.2 minutes. He shot just .426 from the field, .750 at the line and made just one of 13 3's he attempted. He averaged 5.4 points and an incredible—considering the number of minutes he played—7.8 assists, 12th best in the NBA. Even more startling was his efficiency at guard, his 620 assists were exactly five times higher than his 124 turnovers.

Harter wasn't impressed, but Harter was fired midway through the Hornets' second season, January 31, 1990, and replaced with Gene Littles, who coached the next season and a half. Nearly five years after taking over the Hornets, Littles was named interim coach of the Denver Nuggets after Dan Issel quit, January 15, 1995.

Muggsy, who started in 65 of 81 games in 1989-90, averaged 9.4 points and 10.7 assists, fourth in the NBA, but Charlotte struggled to a 19-63 record despite playing in front

Muggsy drives past a much taller opponent.
Courtesy of the Charlotte Hornets
Photo by Greg Forwerck

of one sellout crowd after another at the Charlotte Coliseum. Through 1994-95, the Hornets had filled the 23,698-seat arena in 282 of 287 home games, leading the NBA in attendance in six of its first seven seasons.

In 1990-91, Charlotte went 26-56, as Muggsy averaged 7.0 points and 8.3 assists.

Then the Hornets hired Allan Bristow as head coach, July 23, 1991, and the franchise, as well as Muggsy's role in it, was changed forever. Bristow, a 6-foot-7 forward, played in the NBA with Philadelphia, San Antonio, Utah and Dallas. He was an assistant coach for one season at San Antonio, then for six seasons with Denver, before he joined Charlotte as Vice President of Basketball Operations. The Hornets were his first head coaching job.

And he just loved Muggsy.

"I was in love with the way he played," Bristow said in 1995. "One is, I've always been a big advocate of the up-tempo game. He's always had the ability to create and to push the ball up quickly. Secondly, I always liked little guys. When I was in Denver, I was involved in getting Michael Adams."

Adams, who is listed at 5-10, was a star in Denver in between two tenures with the Washington Bullets. On August 2, 1994, the Hornets acquired Adams from the Bullets for second round draft picks in 1996 and '97. With Charlotte, Adams is Muggsy's back-up, a testament as to how good the Hornets have become. Adams' career scoring average is 15.4, and he holds the NBA record for consecutive games with a three-pointer (79), and is first all-time in treys attempted (2,816) and second in treys made (935).

Another indication of the Hornets' strength in '94-95 was that they had obtained former Boston Celtics center Robert Parish, a certain Hall of Famer, to back up Mourning.

But the two days that changed the Hornets franchise were the 1991 and '92 Draft Days, when they used their No. 1 and No. 2 lottery picks to grab Johnson and Mourning. Simply, they are among the NBA's best at their two positions, power forward and center, and Charlotte's position in the standings hasn't been the same since they arrived.

Under Bristow, the Hornets were 31-51, 44-38 and 41-41 in '93-94 despite the lengthy absences of both Johnson and Mourning. Johnson missed 31 games with a lower back sprain, and Mourning 22 with a torn calf muscle and a sprained ankle.

With both healthy in '94-95, Charlotte flourished.

Muggsy has blossomed under Bristow. His scoring average climbed in each of Bristow's first four seasons, from 7.0 to 8.9, 10.0, 10.8 and 11.1.

There's no debate whether Muggsy can start in the NBA. He started 235 of 236 games in the last three seasons, and his play the past two seasons has been the best of his life: more points, more assists, more steals, consistently fewer turnovers, improved field goal shooting, the best foul shooting of his career and the increasing number of wins Charlotte keeps registering. The Hornets' 50-32 record in '94-95 was their best ever.

"If you look at what he's done the last year and a half, he's been playing great," Bristow said in January of '95.

Bristow offered his perspective of Muggsy's height: "Deficiencies are magnified with small players. It's easy to say Muggsy is too short. I think if you look at any player in this league, except for a Magic Johnson and a Larry Bird, everybody has some deficiency."

And long, long ago, Muggsy learned to accept his deficiency. He was 5-3, he always will be 5-3, and he has never let it keep him from playing the game he loves so dearly. Watch him during a game and see how much he enjoys playing. He leads the NBA in smiles.

His home life, whenever the NBA schedule allows him to be home, is a pleasure. He and his wife, Kimberly, have two daughters, Tyisha (twelve) and Brittney (seven), and a three-year-old son, Tyrone Jr. "The kids understand that Daddy has to play a game," he said. "They know they can't go to games on weekdays. My seven year old understands. My three year old is coming around."

For other kids, he holds an annual summer charity game called "Reading and Roundball," in Baltimore, of course. He'll always remember what he went through growing up there.

He was asked how he'd like to be remembered. He said, "as a guy who really worked hard, who gave it his all, and who enjoyed the game. As someone who saw opportunities and took advantage, and somebody who believed."

Now everybody believes.

Statistics

Muggsy Bogues

Collegiate

Season	Team	G	Avg Pts	Avg Asts	Avg Reb	FG Pct	FT Pct
1983-84	Wake Forest	32	1.2	1.7	0.7	.304	.692
'84-85	Wake Forest	29	6.6	7.1	2.4	.500	.682
'85-86	Wake Forest	29	11.3	8.4	3.1	.455	.730
'86-87	Wake Forest	29	14.8	9.5	3.8	.500	.806

NBA

Season	Team	G	Avg Pts	Avg Asts	Avg Reb	Avg Stl	FG Pct	Ft Pct	3 Pt Pct
1987-88	Washington	79	5.0	5.1	1.7	1.6	.390	.784	.188
'88-89	Charlotte	79	5.4	7.8	2.1	1.4	.426	.750	.077
'89-90	Charlotte	81	9.4	10.7	2.6	2.0	.491	.791	.192
'90-91	Charlotte	81	7.0	8.3	2.7	1.7	.460	.796	.000
'91-92	Charlotte	82	8.9	9.1	2.9	2.1	.671	.783.	.074
'92-93	Charlotte	81	10.0	8.8	3.7	2.0	.453	833	.231
'93-94	Charlotte	77	10.8	10.1	4.1	1.7	.471	.806	.167
'94-95	Charlotte	78	11.1	8.7	3.3	1.3	.477	.889	.200

CHAPTER 3

Mister 5-7

Charlotte Hornets center Alonzo Mourning—who is 6-foot-10—ripped off the rebound of a missed shot by the Golden State Warriors last winter. Then he made a mistake, bringing the ball down to waist level.

That allowed Golden State's Keith "Mister" Jennings—who is 5-foot-7—to clamp his hands on the ball and try to wrest it free. He couldn't. But neither could Mourning.

Jump ball. "The only thing I was thinking about was if he was going to hold the ball down, I was going to try to steal it," Keith said.

If 15 inches isn't the largest discrepancy on a jump ball in the NBA, it's certainly up there.

Mourning won the tap. Keith won respect. He's been doing that for a long time. When you're 5-7, sometimes you even have to earn respect from your own teammates.

In his junior season at East Tennessee State, the coaching staff decided to test their players' vertical leap by having them jump next to a measuring board. Keith jumped and couldn't reach the lowest measure on the board. His teammates thought it was hysterical.

"The other players were laughing," said East Tennessee State Coach Les Robinson—now the coach at North Carolina State. "Then it hit me. I got out the stats from last season. He'd come in third in rebounding on the team."

Robinson looked at his players and said, "Isn't that funny, guys? That makes you look sick. He finishes third in rebounding and can't even get up on the board."

Keith found a way to get long rebounds by out-hustling others, just as he found a way into an NBA lineup at 5-7. "I thought he'd make it," Keith's younger brother, Kirk said. "I just knew. He was very gifted and he has the will to win."

Their dad, Ken, saw that same determination in Keith growing up in Culpeper, Virginia: "He said, basically, you can do what you want, if you've got the heart. You can make your own breaks."

Ken Jennings, who is 5-foot-7—Keith's mom, Zerlene, is 5-3—knows firsthand the resistance Keith got trying to play basketball, a tall man's sport. "I was always told I was too small, or I was too short," said Ken, who still lives in Culpeper and works for the Virginia Department of Transportation. "All through high school, I said, 'Give me a chance.' That's basically all my sons asked for. I always heard I was too short. I even had one of my coaches tell me."

Ken, now 53, was a spot starter at George Washington Carver High School. He was in his late 20s as his kids grew up, and he played lots of sandlot basketball, especially on weekends when his wife, a nurse, worked at Culpeper County Hospital.

"So when I went out to play, Keith would come along," Ken said. "He was four or five years old. While I was playing a game, he'd play with the ball, bounce it on the sidelines.

After the games were over, me or my friends would pick him up, or my other two boys, and let them try to throw the ball in."

Actually, Keith dunked the ball at age five. But he had help. Washington Bullets Hall of Fame center Wes Unseld, who was dedicating a new gym in Culpeper, lifted Keith up to the basket with one hand for Keith's first jam. His second was in college. He's still working on No. 3.

"He was a gifted kid," Ken said. "He had the talent, especially in baseball, at an early age."

Keith, 26, is three years younger than Ken Jr., whose nickname is "Man," and four years older than Kirk. Two sisters, Cherrie and Karen, are 32 and 30, respectively.

At early ages, triumphs are measured in small doses. "Man," Keith and Kirk were highly competitive. "They would get upset and angry, but they were always good to each other," their mom, Zerlene, said. "Keith would come in and say, 'Man beat me in basketball again.'

"I'd say, 'Try again.'

"Then one day, he came in and said, 'Mom, I beat him.'"

Keith (right) with his brothers Kirk (left) and Ken Jr. (middle)

Zerlene remembers another conversation with Keith: "He was always ambitious. It's always been his goal to get to the highest level of whatever he was trying. When he was in high school he said, 'I'm going to make the pros someday.'

"I said, 'Just go for it.'

"He said, 'I want to do my best, Mom.'

"I said, 'That's all you can do.'"

Keith's childhood was perfectly normal. "Real good kid," his father said. "He wasn't bad, but mischievous. Boy things. Like not listening when he was told to go to bed. When you told him to stop doing something, he went to the limit."

That's how Keith got his nickname. He was six when he and his dad went to a Pop Warner Minor League football practice. After a couple hours, Ken was ready to go. He told Keith. Then he told Keith. Then he told Keith again. Then he was yelling, "Keith, come on."

Keith didn't pay much attention: "I was playing with my friends. I just ignored him. He kept calling, 'Keith.'"

Finally, Ken took a harsher posture: "MISTER Jennings, get over here!"

"All of my friends thought that was neat," Keith said. "They all had a strange expression on their faces: 'Mister, where does Mister come from?'"

The name remains.

Keith's athletic talent surfaced at a very early age. "Keith was always a little above kids his age," his dad said.

Keith knew: "When I was six, seven or eight, I was so much better than the other kids my age, that it became second nature for me. I played other sports, and everything came pretty easy to me."

His boyhood heroes were point guards Isiah Thomas and Mark Jackson in basketball, and, of all people, fullback Earl Campbell in football. "Earl Campbell was my favorite," Keith said. "I wanted to be just like him. He'd get tackled and get up real slow like he was hurt, then he'd come back and run harder the next time."

But the sport he performed best in was baseball. "I wanted to be a professional athlete, but I didn't know if it would be in basketball or baseball," he said. He was a shortstop/pitcher in high school and good enough to attract major league scouts.

He also loved football, playing halfback and cornerback. His father, though, ended his schoolboy football career, believing that in doing so he might have saved his son's life: "I had to stop him from playing. He was getting hurt all the time. He didn't want to stop. Three Friday nights in a row, he wound up in the hospital. He hurt his back, his neck, his jaw. I gave him no choice. He wasn't going to play football anymore."

Keith acquiesced: "It seemed like every time something would happen. I hurt my ribs. I had a concussion."

He wasn't heavily recruited in basketball, getting offers from Emory & Henry (Virginia), VMI (Virginia Military Institute) and Fairmont State (West Virgina).

But, thanks to a basketball fan Keith didn't know, he wound up on scholarship at East Tennessee State instead.

An East Tennessee fan named Howard Johnson had a daughter who lived in Culpeper. He saw Keith play and was mesmerized. So he called up East Tennessee Coach Les Robinson. "He kept telling us about a kid from Culpeper, Virginia," Robinson said. "People are always telling you about players. You check them out. Keith was 5-6 (then). We weren't going to make a beeline to Culpeper."

One night, walking off the court after a home game, Robinson was again greeted by Howard Johnson, who offered to send him clips about Keith. "I went in the locker room, and I told my assistant, Dave Hanners, I said, 'He [Howard Johnson] has been talking to us about Keith for a year. We need to check him out.'"

Hanners did. He came back and told Robinson, "The kid can play."

So Robinson sent another assistant, Alan LeForce—now the head coach at East Tennessee State—to scout Keith. Robinson reported: "He came back and said, 'Les, he can play, but he's awfully small. He doesn't necessarily play point guard. He's a 5-6 Oscar Robertson.'"

Les Robinson decided to check out Keith himself. "I watched Mister play a quarter," Robinson said. "I said to my brother, 'We're taking him. This guy can play.'"

Keith didn't disappoint. "He's very skilled, very talented," Robinson said. "Everybody sees the court, but not everybody can thread the needle. That's a gift. It's a natural: getting the ball to the right place at the right time. He has that knack. And you don't take the ball away from him. We didn't know he could shoot well because he was always passing the ball. I had to yell at him, 'Shoot it!'"

He did. He shot three-point field goals better than almost everyone in the history of college basketball, a talent he's carried over quite successfully to the NBA. Through the 1993-94 season, he ranked second in NCAA career three-point shooting (.493), behind only Tony Bennett (.497) of Wisconsin-Green Bay, who has also played in the NBA. Keith's .592 percentage in 1990-91 is the third best single season ever behind Glenn Tropf of Holy Cross (.634) and Sean Wightman of Western Michigan (.632).

Keith is also third in career assists (983), ninth in career assist average (7.74), fourth in career steals (334) and 16th in career steals average (2.63) in all-time NCAA history.

His scoring average rose in each of his seasons in college, from 12.9 to 14.5 to 14.8 and to 20.1 as a senior, when he shot .596 from the field and .895 at the foul line, and scored a career-high 37 against Marshall in a 99-88 win.

His improvement was reflected by the success of East Tennessee State. The Buccaneers went 14-15 in Keith's freshman year, then 20-11, 27-7 and 28-5, when they won the Southern Conference Tournament and then narrowly lost to Iowa, 76-73, in the first round of the NCAA Tournament.

Keith won the Naismith Award as the nation's best player ·
under six feet.

"I think height is one of the most overrated factors in
basketball because so many of the great players have not been
tall," Les Robinson said. "Jerry West, Oscar Robertson,
Michael Jordan. Those are not tall players. Height is important, but the game has become so mobile. Being fluid is so
important."

But, as scouts are wont to say, guards are a dime a dozen.
And not one NBA club wanted a 5-7 guard on Draft Day of
1991.

"When he wasn't drafted, it hurt the whole family," Keith's
younger brother Kirk said.

Ignoring Keith's stats were one thing. But he'd played—and
held his own—against some of the nation's top guards: Kenny
Anderson, Chris Corchiani, Sherman Douglas, Mookie Blaylock
and Bimbo Coles. Keith, in fact, was a 1991 Consensus Second
Team All-American. The other Consensus All-Americans were:

First Team—Kenny Anderson, Jimmy Jackson, Larry
Johnson, Billy Owens and Shaquille O'Neal. Second Team—
Stacey Augmon, Christian Laettner, Eric Murdock and Steve
Smith. All found their way into the NBA.

Keith "Mister" Jennings would, too. Eventually.

First, he had a reality check. He was not selected in the
1991 NBA Draft. It's a startling blow to a player's self-con-
fidence when he is literally left out of the loop. "I just had to
listen to a lot of people tell me I wouldn't have made it
anyway," he said. "My agent in Chicago, Herb Rudoy, said
I'd still make it. He still believed in me. He said, 'If you didn't
get drafted, you didn't get drafted.'"

So Keith played a season with the Jacksonville Hooters in
the summer United States Basketball League, a cut below the
top minor league, the Continental Basketball Association
(CBA). From there, Rudoy got Keith a tryout with the Indiana
Pacers in 1991, an experience which only humbled Keith
even more. "I thought I was ready, but I played awful," he

said. "That was probably the worst basketball I ever played. I wasn't shooting well. I wasn't making proper decisions on the break. My legs were cramping up, and that's the first time that ever happened. I wasn't in good shape."

He played so poorly in the three-day camp that he didn't follow through on another one: "I was supposed to go and try out with Milwaukee, but I had played so terribly, I didn't."

Instead, he accepted an offer from Germany. This was his thinking: "Let me go there and get focused."

And he did, playing on a team named Brandt Hagen in Hagen, Germany. "It was different, but it was okay," he said.

The presence of his younger brother, Kirk, who was in the U.S. Army and stationed in Germany just two hours away, helped him cope with life in a foreign country.

But it was his play with his foreign team back in the U.S. which jump-started his NBA career. In the middle of its season, his German team toured Northern California, playing games at California-Berkeley, San Francisco, Santa Clara, the University of Pacific, Nevada-Reno and Sacramento.

On the tour, Keith got two breaks. One was that Ed Gregory and Donn Nelson of the Warriors front office decided to scout a game on a night Keith went wild, scoring 40 points and getting 14 rebounds and eight assists. Break No. 2 was that Donn Nelson knew one of the German team's owners, Charles Bretz, and invited the German team to watch a Warriors' practice.

Keith worked out with a couple Warriors, and Golden State decided to follow Keith's continuing season in Germany. "We had liked Keith out of college," Donn Nelson said. "I scouted him when his German team played Cal-Berkeley, and I really liked him then, too."

Donn's dad, Coach and General Manager Don Nelson, liked Keith enough to give him a chance. After Keith's season in Germany finished, the Warriors invited him to play on their summer league team in the Rocky Mountain Review in Salt Lake City, Utah.

Having Tim Hardaway, an NBA All-Star at six feet, on the Warriors certainly had an impact on Nelson's thinking. "Early in my career, I didn't like small guards," he said during the '94-95 season. "Now there seems to be a place for them. The three-point shot has been a factor, for sure. Also, more teams play an automatic switch for defensive help. Now I'm a fan of the small guard, but he has to have multiple skills. He has to be able to shoot the ball from the outside. He's got to be a non-turnover player, and he's got to be quick and be able to defend, in his own way, with his speed and quickness. The most important thing is penetration. He drives into seams in the defense. He has to create shots, because he can get into areas bigger people can't."

Like onto an NBA basketball court.

Still smarting from his poor tryout camp the year before, Keith went home to Culpeper on a mission to prepare for the Rocky Mountain Review.

"I didn't work as hard as I could have the first time," he said. "This was going to be different. I wanted to be better prepared. I really didn't want to go overseas again."

At home, his mom woke him up at six a.m. four days out of seven each week to run two and a half miles. He shot 200 to 300 jump shots daily. He worked out with weights. And he played every single night, either on the playgrounds or in the high school gym at Culpeper.

In Utah, he played with Latrell "Spree" Sprewell, Byron Houston, Vic Alexander and Tyrone Hill—all destined to be his teammates on the Warriors. Keith played well, averaging eight points and six assists, and was invited to the Warriors' veterans' camp. "I was getting closer to my dream," he said. "I knew I didn't want to just get to the camp. I wanted to go all the way. I just played really hard. I didn't let anyone intimidate me."

But he did have to make an attitude adjustment, a quick one. To make the Warriors, he couldn't be in awe of marquee teammates, players such as NBA All-Stars Tim Hardaway and

Chris Mullin. "You realize they're great athletes, but after you get to play with them a little while, you learn you can do the same things they do," he said.

As he continued to play well in training camp, the opportunity to make the team became tantalizingly closer. Then Don Nelson shook him up one day near the end of camp: "I thought I was playing well enough to make the team, but Coach said, 'Little man, you're going to play yourself out of a position.' He said I wasn't doing the things I did that got me into that position.

"A bell went off in my head. I wasn't playing aggressive. I'm glad he told me that."

The drama went down to the final day of camp and the Warriors' final cut. "It was torture," Keith said.

He made the team. Then came the real, physical torture.

Life in the NBA was rosy for Keith in his 1992-93 rookie season for a little more than two weeks. While getting 17 minutes a night, he was averaging a healthy 8.6 points and 2.9 assists through eight games. He scored 22 in a win over Miami. Two nights later, in a game against Orlando, his world fell apart.

He guesses the dreaded injury may have actually happened while he was a junior in college. In a game against Marshall, he felt a twinge in his right knee. He played on. The team won in overtime, and, after the game, X-rays were taken. "The bones looked healthy," Keith said. "There was no indication of a torn anterior cruciate ligament (ACL)."

The knee didn't bother him in his senior year in college nor during his season in Germany. But in the Warriors' sixth game of the '92-93 season, the knee pushed out. "I went to plant my right leg, and the knee kind of hyperextended," he said. "But it was my first year in the NBA. I wasn't going to let an injury stop me."

It didn't, immediately. Keith went out the next game and scored his then career high against Miami. In the next game at Orlando, though, he hyperextended it again. "I walked it

Keith Jennings lets it fly.
Courtesy of the Golden State Warriors
Photo by Sam Forencich

off, and it actually felt all right," he said. "Then two minutes later, I made a move to the basket. I heard the pop. I thought I twisted it."

Two teammates carried him into the locker room. "The doctor thought it was a bad sprain," Keith said.

"The next night, I was supposed to start against Muggsy Bogues in Charlotte. But when I went to warm up, I told Coach there was no way. It would've been my first start. It was on TNT [cable TV], and I was going to play against the guy who paved the way for me."

Keith returned to Oakland and was examined by another doctor. The doctor didn't tell Keith his diagnosis, opting instead to tell Don Nelson first.

"He called me into his office," Keith said. "I thought I was going to have a little scope [arthroscopic surgery]. I have never been injured. Never. The worst thing that happened was I sprained an ankle badly, but I played anyway against Wake Forest.

"Coach told me:

'Keith, the doctor told me you ripped your ACL.'

"My jaw dropped," Keith said. "I cried right in front of him. I couldn't believe it was happening to me in my first year in the league. Here I was on top of the world. Coach was giving me more minutes and showing more confidence in me and then—boom—it all ends just like that."

Nelson, though, told Keith that although his season had ended, his career with the Warriors hadn't. They did not release him.

But careers have been jeopardized or lost because of a torn anterior cruciate ligament, one of two central ligaments which support the knee. The injury denied Danny Manning of the Suns one and a half seasons because of two separate tears, one in each knee. The injury sidetracked top scorer Bernard King for two seasons, before he overcame it and returned to the NBA.

Once again, Keith was confronted with a defining moment: "I definitely went through a 'Why me?' stage. I couldn't believe what had happened. But eventually I had to accept it and throw myself into my rehab."

He started by lifting weights, then added jogging and running under the supervision of Warriors Strength and Conditioning Coach Mark Grabow. "It was very hard," Keith said. "I had to get the muscles in my leg strong."

He was driven to return to the little piece of NBA real estate he'd worked so hard to get. Though he didn't play for seven and a half months following the injury, he made it back, all the way back.

"He had a tough time, but he came back like a champ," Tim Hardaway said. "What can I say? He's an extraordinary guy to be that small and come back from an injury like that."

Keith played in 76 games with the Warriors in 1993-94, averaging 14.4 minutes, 5.7 points, 2.9 assists against just 0.9 turnovers, 1.2 rebounds and 0.9 steals. He started in two games. The first was a special one, a year after he was supposed to make his first start against the same man: Muggsy Bogues of the Charlotte Hornets.

He'd met Muggsy the year before. "I was looking forward to meeting him, but I didn't know really what to expect because you could kind of look at it in two different ways," Keith said. "I didn't know if I would offend him by being in the NBA because I'm a small guy like he is, or if he would be happy that another small man had made it. Muggsy was just super, right off the bat. He said, 'Congratulations and welcome to the League.' He's cool."

Keith was, too. He knew he belonged in the greatest basketball league in the world. "I think the more you get to play in the league, the more confident you become," he said. "1993-94 was my first full year. If I made a mistake, Coach Nelson would get on me, and it was hard. Now, I don't let missed shots get to me. If I make a mistake, I don't get upset. The experience really helps me out."

So does weak-side help. When a guard posts Keith up, Keith does his best to force him out as far away from the basket as he can without getting called for a foul. He'll gamble on a steal if the player turns a shoulder. "I try to fight him until there's a double team," Keith said.

On defense at the other end of the court, Keith says his job is: "To be a pain in the ass, hassle him up the court, make it uneasy for him to bring the ball up."

Keith's '94-95 season was a smash from Day One. In the opener against San Antonio, he played 26 minutes, hitting a crucial three-pointer in a 123-118 win. "Spree drove the middle and drew everyone with him," Keith said. "He kicked it out to me. I was so wide open."

Through the season, while the injury-ravaged Warriors self-destructed after three controversial trades—Billy Owens to Miami for Rony Seikaly; Chris Webber to Washington for Tom Gugliotta and three draft picks; and then Gugliotta to the Minnesota Timberwolves for rookie Donyell Marshall—Keith excelled, becoming a spot starter after mid-January.

He finished 10th in the NBA in foul shooting (.876) and 10th in the league in assist to turnover ratio (3.11 to 1). He averaged 7.4 points, 4.7 assists against 1.5 turnovers and 1.9 rebounds in 21.5 minutes a night, and he scored a career high of 23 against the Denver Nuggets, April 22, 1995.

"He's been doing an excellent job every night," Tim Hardaway said before a game against the Knicks last February.

The losing, however, was killing everyone, Don Nelson and Keith included. Nelson was hospitalized with viral pneumonia, and later resigned as coach and general manager. Five months later, he was named new coach of the Knicks, and he's certain to get fewer losses in New York than he did with the Warriors. Keith endured them all, as Golden State finished 26-56.

"The losing is tough," Keith said in mid-season. "I haven't been on a losing team really like this, consistently losing, since my freshman year in high school when we were 6 and 16. This team has had so much bad luck, but you can't blame it on that. You can't blame it on chemistry. You can't blame it on people getting hurt. There's nothing you can blame it on.

We're just playing bad basketball. No one likes to lose. I don't like to lose. I try to play hard. I try to do my best, do something positive for this team so we can win."

Keith Jr. at six months.

He tried, but the Warriors chose not to make him one of the eight players they protected in the NBA Expansion Draft, June 24, 1995, and the neophyte Toronto Raptors made him their fourth selection. The dramatic change of scenery for Keith, his fiancee, Bernadette, and their now one-year-old son, Keith Jr., is a welcome one because Keith is anything but finished with what he hopes to accomplish in the NBA.

"Some people believe the small man should just be used to give a team a spark," he said. "I feel the small player can play heavy minutes."

This one does.

Statistics

Keith Jennings

Collegiate

Season	Team	G	Avg Pts	Avg Ast	Avg Reb	FG Pct	FT Pct	3 Pt Pct
1987-88	E. Tenn St.	29	12.9	6.3	4.1	.489	.826	.382
'88-89	E. Tenn St.	31	14.5	6.5	3.7	.510	.847	.447
'89-90	E. Tenn St.	34	14.8	8.7	3.9	.574	.877	.496
'90-91	E. Tenn St.	33	20.1	9.1	3.9	.596	.895	.592

NBA

Season	Team	G	Avg Pts	Avg Ast	Avg Reb	Avg Stl	FG Pct	FT Pct	3 Pt Pct
1992-93	Golden St.	8	8.6	2.9	1.4	0.5	.595	.788	.556
'93-94	Golden St.	76	5.7	2.9	1.2	0.9	.404	.833	.371
'94-95	Golden St.	80	7.4	4.7	1.9	1.2	.447	.876	.368

Greg
5-7

Greg Grant was in basketball purgatory in Orlando, Florida, last November and loving every second of it.

He was a member of the Orlando Magic, sort of.

Orlando is the now team in the NBA and the franchise of the future as well, a foundation built on the hulking strength of Shaquille O'Neal and the grace and unlimited potential of point guard Penny Hardaway.

The Magic made headlines in the off season by acquiring a free agent from the three-time NBA champion Chicago Bulls.

His name was Grant. Horace Grant, one of the league's outstanding power forwards and a perfect complement for Shaq.

Greg Grant? What in the world was a 5-foot-7 point guard from a Division III college doing on the NBA team of the '90s?

Greg Grant might still be working in a fish market today if basketball coach Kevin Bannon hadn't walked through the door of the Crab Shack in Trenton, New Jersey, some nine years ago. "My cholesterol level went down 20 percent recruiting Greg," laughed Bannon, then the coach of Trenton State and now the head coach at Rider College in Lawrenceville, New Jersey.

Bannon and Greg hit it off immediately, maybe because they shared a trait: perseverance.

Bannon had tried recruiting Grant out of Trenton High School and failed. Greg took a scholarship to Morris Brown College in Atlanta, played a couple of games and returned to Trenton. "I wasn't even thinking about going back to school," he said.

He couldn't. The real world wouldn't let him. His future wife, Aretha, was pregnant with the first of their two children.

Greg got a job in the shipping department of an air conditioning factory. He got laid off after six months and did construction work with his dad. "I really didn't want to do that," Greg said. "It was too hard."

He found a new job at the Crab Shack where he sold and cleaned fish.

But he kept playing basketball. In a summer league, he was scoring 42 a game.

Bannon watched him and decided to recruit him again. "I just loved the way he played in high school, and he was tearing up the summer leagues," Bannon said. "He was enormously talented."

So Bannon went fishing in a fish store and hooked Greg. "I told him I'd love to go back to school, and that I missed basketball," Greg said. "My goal was to be a professional basketball player coming out of high school, but another goal became to get an education so I wouldn't have to work like I had."

But in reality, he worked harder than that to make it to the NBA. He had to.

The odds of any college player making it to the NBA are astronomical. The odds of a 5-7 player reaching that destination are even greater. And Greg's chances were much worse than that because he sought to make the jump to the NBA from a Division III college. There are no scholarships in Division III, and players there rarely spring from obscurity into an NBA spotlight. Or even into a single NBA game. Since 1974, when small colleges split into Division II (with scholarships) and Division III, only four Division III players before Greg had ever made it to the NBA—Derrick Rowland (Potsdam State, New York), Clinton Wheeler (Wm. Paterson, New Jersey), Michael Harper (North Park, Illinois) and Sam "Bam, The Franchise" Pellom (Buffalo, New York). Rowland played two games with Milwaukee; Wheeler 87 with Indiana, Miami and Portland; Harper 123 with Portland; and Pellom 196 with Atlanta and Milwaukee.

Those were Greg's odds. But once his spirit was renewed by Bannon, he began his mission again, one born of childhood dreams watching the Philadelphia 76ers on TV. "I was a diehard 76er fan," he said. One day he'd play for them, though that hardly seemed plausible when he was cut as a sophomore from Trenton High School's JV team. "They didn't think I was good enough," Greg said. "I believe it was my height. It hurt. It was real bad. When you're young, you take things personally. That was almost the end of the world for me."

Not quite. A few players and friends spoke to the coach, Tom Smith, and he reconsidered and put Greg on the team. "He gave me another shot," Greg said. "But it wasn't the same as being originally placed on the team."

The next season, he was the only junior on annual powerhouse Trenton High's 15-man varsity. "I didn't play a lot, but I played," Greg said. "There was so much talent. You didn't play varsity until you're a senior. I was happy. I knew next year, I'd be the man."

Greg surveys the court for Trenton State.
Courtesy of Trenton State College

Just to make sure, Greg drove himself relentlessly. Actually, he'd been doing that long before he was a junior in high school.

Greg was the oldest of five children of Albert and Mary Williams (Albert, his stepfather, helped raise Greg since he was a baby. "He's my only father," Greg said.) Albert had his own construction company. Mary worked as a nurse's aide.

In high school, Greg ran cross country because he thought it gave him an advantage. "It gave me an edge," he said. "I was in tremendous shape. I was No. 3 runner on the team. I could have been All-American or All-State if I worked on it in the summer."

But summers were meant for basketball. And basketball was becoming his life, a good life because he could play, even though he was 5-foot-7. Damn what people said about his chances.

"I can't tell you the first time somebody said, 'You're too short,' but I always heard the comments," he said.

"'He's fast enough, but he's too short.'

"I always heard it. I heard it in junior high, I heard it in high school and I heard it in college.

"'He's too short.'

"I got tired of it real quick. I think a lot of athletes say when people put you down, it drives you. I wanted to be the first 5-7 guy to ever play in the NBA, but Spud and Muggsy (Monte Towe, too) beat me to it. That was the determination I had. I said, 'I'm going to do it! I'm going to do it!'

"All those people said it couldn't be done. I did crazy stuff to get myself over the edge. I would run four miles to college in the morning and run home after practice. I'd run in the rain, run in the snow. It never really stopped me from doing more. I wanted to do more than anyone else. I couldn't see myself practicing for two hours and saying, 'That's it.' I had to practice three hours. After the others would leave, I'd go around for another hour just to say I did something more than anyone else today. That gave me the edge. It's tough to get up and run in the snow. But I always knew one day it would pay off and one day it did."

He starred his senior year in high school, averaging 22 points a game. He led his team to the Central Jersey Finals and led his county in scoring.

He expected to be recruited by major colleges, but no offers came, not a single one from Division I. Trenton State showed interest but he chose to go to Division II Morris Brown College in Atlanta. "I thought I needed to get away," he said.

Half a year later, he knew he needed to go home. He did. And he got his second chance at college a year and a half later.

Bannon couldn't wait: "I saw him play at Trenton High School. There was a lot of talk about a presidential backcourt. They had a kid named John Adams and Greg Grant. Adams was 5-7, too. I just fell in love with Greg's energy. One of the things people always bring up is that he never gets tired. He just played at an unbelievable energy level. He always would play his man full court defense whether his other teammates were or not. He was relentless. He just loves to compete. To him, that just sent a message to his opponent: 'This is the way it's going to be tonight.'

"I wouldn't want to play against him: that tough, that quick, that fast, and he just never ever tired."

So Bannon threw out his playbook when Greg arrived: "We used to play ball control at a slower pace. Once Greg came on board, I threw that philosophy out of the window. I changed my coaching strategy. We did anything possible to get the other team into an up and down game because he would dominate."

And he did.

In his sophomore season at Trenton State, he averaged 28.5 points, 4.0 rebounds, 3.0 steals and 2.8 assists, and set a school record by scoring 51 points in a game at Montclair State. He shot a robust .484 from the field, an even higher percentage on 3's, .518, and .777 at the line.

Then he did better.

Greg drives to the basket.
Courtesy of Trenton State College

As a junior, he led the Lions to a 26-4 season. He broke his own record by scoring 52 points in a 108-81 win at Wilmington College, Delaware, January 18, 1988. Besides finishing second in the nation in Division III in scoring

(30.6)—Matt Hancock of Colby (Maine) was first at 31.6—he shot .562 from the field, .495 on 3's, and .838 at the line.

He set an NCAA Division III Tournament record by scoring 85 points in two games: 40 points, along with nine steals, in an 87-50 rout of Bridgewater College (Virginia), then a Trenton State Packer Hall record 45 in an 82-72 win against Emory & Henry College (Virginia) as the Lions won the NCAA Division III South Atlantic Regional Tournament. He, of course, was named the Tournament's Most Outstanding Player.

Host Hartwick (in Oneonta, New York) took out the Lions in the NCAA Quarterfinals, 84-69, but Greg, who scored 24 in defeat, vowed the next day: "We'll work very hard to get another chance at winning the national championship."

Greg was named a Division III All-American, and he was the only non-Division I selection for the United Press International Small American Team.

Then he did better.

In his senior year, the Lions went 30-2, the best record of any college team in any division—Ball State led Division I at 29-3, and University of California-Riverside's 30-4 was best in Division II. Greg scored 40 or more 10 times, and he was named Division III College Player of the Year after leading the country (Division III) in scoring at 32.6 points a game and scoring a still Division III record 1,044 points in a single season. His 1,044 points also made him the No. 1 single season college scorer in New Jersey history, eclipsing U.S. Senator Bill Bradley's mark at Princeton (936). For the season, Greg shot .522 from the field, .812 at the line and .409 on 3's, and averaged 4.6 steals, 3.8 assists and 2.3 rebounds. His career point total (2,611) is also No. 1 in New Jersey and sixth in Division III history.

But he lost the one game he wanted the most, the Division III National Championship, to Wisconsin-Whitewater, 94-86. Greg, who scored 35 in the loss, would be named Tournament MVP, but he was crying at the buzzer of his last college game. His teammates embraced him on the sidelines. "It was a great run," he said.

But Greg's run was far from over. He focused on the NBA. "There are certain ways you can face obstacles in your life," Bannon said. "Greg's way was to meet obstacles head on. He was never an excuse guy. He was a guy who always wanted to find a way. Find a way to do it. As a coach, I wish you could bottle that."

Bannon, who was best man at Greg's wedding, will always have a place in Greg's heart. "He's like a father to me," Greg said.

As a father would, Bannon did everything he could to promote Greg: making countless phone calls, editing tapes and pursuing NBA scouts. "It's one thing to get people to see you, but you have to make the most of it," Bannon said.

Greg did.

He performed well enough in post-season all-star games (in Portsmouth, Virginia, in Orlando, and in one in Japan) to elicit the interest of the Phoenix Suns. They made him the 52nd pick in second round of the 1989 NBA Draft.

He'd made it. But typically, that wasn't enough for him. He played in the L.A. Summer Pro League and averaged 23 points, continuing to work on his game, specifically to increase his shooting range and improve his defense.

He appeared in 67 games with the Suns, averaging 3.1 points, 2.5 assists and 10 minutes.

The Suns let him go, and Greg was signed by the Knicks as an unrestricted free agent the following season, averaging 1.2 points, 0.9 assists and 4.9 minutes in just 22 games.

The Knicks released him, and Indiana signed him as a free agent on September 6, 1991, only to waive him October 29, just before the 1991-92 season started. Charlotte signed him just two days later to back up 5-3 Muggsy Bogues. "We got to be real close," Greg said. "We went through the same thing. I know how tough it was for him to make it, as tough as it was for me. We have something in common. I think all little guys do."

The Hornets used Greg in 13 games before waiving him on December 9, 1991. That wasn't bad for him, because the team he'd grown up rooting for, the Philadelphia 76ers, signed him as a free agent 13 days later. For the '91-92 season, he averaged 3.3 points, 3.2 assists and a healthy 13.1 minutes.

In 72 games with Philadelphia the next year, he averaged 2.7 points, 2.9 assists and 13.8 minutes. He had two double-doubles, 12 points and 11 assists against the Celtics and 10 points and 10 assists at Phoenix. He tied his career high of 15 points and had a career high seven rebounds in a game against Atlanta. How does a 5-7 guard get seven rebounds in an NBA game? "A guard my size can get long rebounds," Greg said. "You just outrun guys to get them. And sometimes you happen to be in the right position."

In a familiar refrain, the 76ers cut him loose, too, and Greg failed to catch on with an NBA team in 1993. So he went down to the Continental Basketball Association (CBA) to work his way back. Playing for the Rapid City (South Dakota) Thrillers, he averaged 7.5 points and 5.5 assists. Then he played in the summer in Canada with Winnipeg in the National Basketball League before getting an invitation to Orlando's 1994-95 training camp.

A longshot? Here's what he faced. He was the fourth point guard in training camp behind Penny Hardaway, newly acquired Brian Shaw and first round draft pick Brooks Thompson. If that wasn't enough of a hurdle, Orlando had 14 guaranteed contracts. The NBA roster is 12.

"When I first got there, the newspaper said they got Greg Grant, who won't be on the team," Greg said. "They were just being honest."

Then he got lucky. Penny decided to hold out. Shaw was injured. And Greg played well enough to beat out Thompson.

Greg lets a jumper fly for the 76ers.
Courtesy of Philadelphia 76ers
Photo by Mike Malcher

He started the Magic's first exhibition game and had 12 points and 10 assists.

Coach Brian Hill said he was not surprised: "I felt right from the beginning he might be a guy who was here right down to the wire. I've always been a fan of his. And Greg's done everything we've asked of him and more. I've got a lot of respect for Greg as a player and a person. He puts tremendous pressure on you defensively, and when he has the ball in his hands, he's tough, too, because he's so quick. I'd love to see him stick here. He's one of those guys you can't help but like."

Not quite enough. Penny ended his holdout and Brian Shaw got healthy. When the season opened, the Magic decided to keep Greg on the roster, anyway, placing him on the injured list (they listed his injury as a hamstring). "For me to be a part of this team, it's a miracle to a lot of people," Greg said. "But not to me."

Sometimes, even miracles aren't enough. When Dennis Scott returned from an injury, November 28, Greg was released. He didn't get to play a single minute in the regular season for the Magic.

"I wish Greg would have stayed," Orlando's 7-1 Assistant Coach/player Tree Rollins said. "Shaq loved him. He knew if Greg had the ball on the break, and Shaq ran downcourt, he'd get the ball for a slam dunk.

"Greg was great just for practice. In practice, he would make Penny's defense improve. If you can stay with a Greg Grant or a Spud Webb or a Charlie Criss and defend those guys off the dribble, you can defend anybody."

Well into the season, Greg was left with few options. He returned to the CBA—a testament of his commitment—with Pittsburgh.

Returning to the CBA can devastate an NBA player. "At first, you don't accept it at all," he said. "If you didn't get upset, you wouldn't call yourself a player. I take it personally when I get released. It's degrading."

Then, as he has his whole career, he re-focused. To get back to the NBA, he had to perform well in the CBA. And he did. He averaged 12.0 points and 9.4 assists in five games with Pittsburgh before he was traded, December 21, 1994, to the Mexico Aztecas, the CBA's newest franchise, in Mexico City.

It was a good trade for Greg because James Blackwell, who'd been called up from Pittsburgh to Charlotte, was released by the Hornets and was ready to take back his starting job.

Greg excelled in Mexico, averaging 17.7 points, 9.8 assists and 1.4 steals, while shooting .920 from the foul line.

"I'm playing well, maybe the best I've played professionally, because I'm getting the minutes [37.1]," he said last February. "This is my team. I can control the game. I can do anything. It's just like high school."

But Mexico City was a long way from Trenton, New Jersey. "It was different, but not too bad," he said. He missed his family, his wife, Aretha, and their two daughters, nine-year-old Amber and two-year-old Jasmine, at home in Hamilton, New Jersey. "I missed the kids, but that was business," he said.

He was fully confident he still had business to do in the NBA, and he knew that next season his chances would improve considerably when expansion teams Vancouver and Toronto join the NBA. That means 24 new roster spots.

He's already shown he can play in the NBA. There he is driving fearlessly into the lane and floating in a layup just over the reach of seven-foot Patrick Ewing. Here he is feeding his teammate Manute Bol—who is 7-foot-7—for a layup. There's Greg slapping high fives with teammate Charles Barkley after another beautiful assist. Barkley loved playing with Grant in Philadelphia, but what was not to like? He delivered pass after pass to him at the right place at the right time. That's how he's carved an NBA career. That's why he got another chance.

"I came up through a lot of negatives," he said. "I came up a little harder because of my size. I always had that negative thing hanging over my head. I was too short to make it. I was too skinny to make it.

"It sounds like a cliché, but if you really want to do something, you can do it. I always knew I was going to be a professional basketball player. I put that in my high school yearbook under "What You Want to Become." That was what I was going to do. I didn't care about money. I didn't care about things. I don't have a trophy. Every trophy I won is at my mom's house. No scrapbook. I don't have a scrapbook. That's not what drives me. What drives me is to be as good as I can. I never wanted to be anything but good and to play with the best players."

He has. And he's played well. That's why two of the biggest guys in pro basketball, 7-1 Shaquille O'Neal and 7-1 Tree Rollins of the Orlando Magic, were rooting for a 5-7 Division III guard to get another chance in the NBA. And he did, after leading the CBA in assists (9.8) and free throw percentage (.919), and finishing seventh in steals (1.6). The Denver Nuggets signed him to a 10-day contract on March 14, 1995, then signed him for the remainder of the season. Greg averaged 2.2 points, 3.1 assists and 10.8 minutes in 14 games, and he had eight points in a late season 102-87 upset of Phoenix as the Nuggets fought their way into the NBA playoffs.

It's tough to keep a good man down.

Statistics

Greg Grant

Collegiate

Season	Team	G	Avg Pts	Avg Ast	Avg Reb	FG Pct	FT Pct	3 Pt Pct
1986-87	Trenton St.	26	28.5	2.8	4.0	.484	.777	.518
'87-88	Trenton St.	27	30.6	3.2	2.6	.562	.838	.495
'88-89	Trenton St.	32	32.6	3.5	2.3	.522	.812	.409

NBA

Season	Team	G	Avg Pts	Avg Ast	Abg Reb	Avg Stl	FG Pct	FT Pct	3 Pt Pct
1989-90	Phoenix	67	3.1	2.5	0.9	0.5	.384	.661	.188
'90-91	New York	22	1.2	0.9	0.5	0.2	.370	.833	.333
'91-92	Char/Phila	68	3.3	3.2	1.0	0.7	.440	.833	.389
'92-93	Philadelphia	72	2.7	2.8	0.9	0.6	.350	.645	.294
'94-95	Denver	14	2.2	3.1	0.6	0.4	.303	.750	.286

CBA

Season	Team	G	Avg Pts	Avg Ast	Avg Reb	Avg Stl	FG Pct	FT Pct	3 Pt Pct
1993-94	Rapid City	41	7.5	5.5	1.6	1.3	.467	.891	.378
'94-95	Pitt/Mexico	33	16.8	9.8	2.3	1.6	.424	.919	.358

Monte
5-7

When Monte Towe was eight years old, he went to see a high school game with his dad at Oak Hill High School. Oak Hill's best player was Earl Brown, who was 6-6 and would go on to play at Purdue University. Monte asked his dad if he would grow to be as tall as him. Corwin "Doc" Towe, who was 5-6, looked at his son and said 'No.' But he also told him that he could still play basketball.

Monte spent the next 15 years proving his father right.

Doc Towe, who got his nickname because his father was a dentist, passed away in 1985 after having seen his son reach the pinnacle of basketball, the NBA. Doc was an electrician for the Public Service Light Company of Indiana. He and his wife, Frances, who taught first grade for a quarter of century, raised four children in Converse, Indiana. Monte was the youngest.

It's been said many times—and portrayed so poetically in the movie "Hoosiers"—that basketball is a part of life in the state of Indiana. "Everybody just assumes you play basketball if you're from Indiana," Monte Towe said.

Monte was an assistant coach in 1994-95 for the Sioux Falls (South Dakota) Skyforce in the Continental Basketball Association (CBA), the minor league feeder system to the NBA. Basketball has taken him to wondrous events and wonderful places, to a national collegiate championship at North Carolina State, and to two years with the Denver Nuggets in the final season of the American Basketball Association and the franchise's first season in the NBA.

Basketball has led him into the profession of coaching. He was an assistant at North Carolina State and at the University of Florida, then head coach in the short-lived Global Basketball Association with the Raleigh (N.C.) Bullfrogs (28-35) and the Fayetteville (N.C.) Flyers, (10-7 when the league folded), and in Venezuela. Basketball has been and always will be part of his life.

"Athletics just took a hold of him," Frances Towe said.

At an early age. By the time he was six, he was reading box scores out of the paper to his parents. "I had the best growing-up experience anybody could have," Monte said. "I was always interested in sports. I don't remember not being interested."

He'd follow his brother Gordon, five years older, around the playgrounds. Gordon wound up playing baseball and football at Oak Hill High School, and graduating from Purdue.

Of course, being talented didn't discourage Monte's interest in athletics. Nor did being fiercely competitive, a fire inside him he's never extinguished. "He plays a lot of tennis now, and he doesn't like to lose," said David Thompson, his long-time friend and former college and pro teammate.

To that mix, he added relentlessness. "Basketball is all he thought of growing up," his mom said. "Lots of times, we didn't know what he was thinking. He just kept practicing and practicing."

Inside, he practiced with a wastebasket and a miniature hoop. Outside, he would dribble a ball three-quarters of a mile to school and back on the sidewalks and streets. "All the other kids watched cartoons on Saturday morning," his mom said. "He never did. He was always practicing basketball."

When he wasn't, he was playing football or baseball or golf. He was adept at all of them. He quarterbacked Oak Hill's football team to two undefeated seasons as the Golden Eagles outscored their competition, 748-20. In baseball, he developed into an outstanding second baseman, and he would play collegiately at North Carolina State. One of his teammates there was Tim Stoddard, who would pitch in the major leagues.

But it was basketball, the sport which would discriminate the most against the inches God had given him, that claimed his heart. Confronted with that obstacle, as well as the unceasing tide of skepticism and negativity which threatened to drown him every time he took a step up to a new level in basketball, he reacted the only way he knew. He worked harder. He took the challenge personally, fully acknowledging the difficulty of his chances of making it in basketball. "I remember my opening game as a seventh grader," he said. "I didn't start. There were bigger players. I didn't look the part. As your stature is, that's the way you're perceived. I don't have a Napoleon complex, but if you're a short person, you have to make people take notice of you. And you have to keep doing it, time after time. And it's magnified in basketball. I almost felt like I had to be a step ahead of the players I played against just to play on a level field."

He drew inspiration from his boyhood idols: "My heroes were basketball players, Rick Mount, Pete Maravich, Bobby Joe Hill. I remember to this day, watching the National Championship game in 1966. I was 12. I was so impressed. Kentucky was a big favorite in that game and Western Texas (now known as UTEP—University of Texas-El Paso) drilled them (72-65).

Monte drives through three defenders in an eighth grade tournament. Monte scored 20 points and his team won 45-31 to take the championship. No. 8 is John Garrett, who grew to be 6-11 and played at Purdue, where he was an All-American.

Courtesy of Ken Hill, Sports Hotline, and Frances Towe
Photo by Don Grubbs

Bobby Joe Hill just controlled the game from the point guard spot. That had an impression on me. The quickness. There was a certain excitement about basketball I'm not sure I've found in other sports."

That evening, he shot baskets outside until 11:30 in his driveway. His father had hooked up a light over the driveway court he'd built for Monte years earlier, allowing Monte to shoot at night. And he did. Many nights. Almost every night. "I loved basketball," he said. "That's what it boiled down to."

His mom first saw him play in the seventh grade: "He said, 'Mother, you don't need to come because I'm not going to start.'

"I said, 'Monte, I'm coming to the gymnasium because you will play.' He went in the second quarter and he immediately began passing and finding the open man. I came home and told my husband, 'Corwin, Monte has a good mind for basketball.'"

Between eighth and ninth grade, on the advice of Oak Hill High School Coach Dave Huffman, Monte began shooting over a ladder to get used to the obstacles he'd encounter when he drove into a lane against taller opposition. "Because of my size, I was going to have to shoot over people much taller than me," Monte said. "He recommended that I get a ladder and put it in front of me. I did it. I think it really did help me."

As a sophomore, he was 5-foot-4 and 126 pounds. He grew to his adult height of 5-7 and 140 pounds by his senior year, 1970-71, when he led his Oak Hill High School team to a 23-4 record and sectional and regional basketball titles.

His mom and dad always sat in the same seats at his home games, the top row under one of the baskets. They saw Monte succeed off the court, as well. He had a 2.9 cumulative grade point average out of 4.0, and he was president of the school's Fellowship of Christian Athletes Chapter.

Averaging 22.9 points a game as a senior, he finished his schoolboy career as Oak Hill's all-time career scoring leader with 1,106 points. But an honor of a lifetime turned out bittersweet.

One of 12 seniors named to represent Indiana in two All-Star games against Kentucky (one in Indianapolis and the second in Louisville), he played little in both games. "It was the first time a coach hadn't shown any confidence in me, and I wondered why," he told reporter Michael Davis of the *Louisville Courier-Journal & Times Magazine* six years later. "He (Coach Angus Nixon) never said anything to me, so I felt the only reason was because of my size."

Size was a concern among college recruiters, too. He desperately wanted to go to Purdue, where his brother and two sisters went, but Purdue wasn't interested. Monte received inquiries from Bradley, Butler and a couple dozen smaller schools. "I didn't think many people thought I could play college basketball," he said.

One who didn't was Norm Sloan, the basketball coach at North Carolina State.

Dick Dickey, a three-time All-American at North Carolina State in the late '40s, had settled in Marion, Indiana, 10 miles from Monte's home. He'd been a teammate of Sloan's in college and the best man at his wedding.

He recommended a few players to Sloan. One was 6-foot-2 John "Crash" Mengelt, whom Sloan passed on. Mengelt went to Auburn and scored 45 in a 91-85 win against North Carolina State, December 5, 1970. Mengelt went on to play 10 seasons in the NBA, 1971-81, with the Cincinnati Royals, the Detroit Pistons, the Chicago Bulls and the Golden State Warriors.

Sloan told Dickey the next guy he recommended he'd take. The next one was Monte Towe.

"Norman asked him how tall I was," Monte related. "Dick said, '5-7.'"

"Norman said, 'I'm running a basketball team not a circus.'"

True to his word, though, Sloan took Towe.

"This boy (Monte) could be just as great as Mengelt, but in a different way," Dickey told local sports writer Ken Hill in a 1971 interview. "He will be a quarterback, but if they start blocking the middle he will keep them honest from the outside. It's a good break for both State and Monte."

Sloan still wasn't sure: "I was still skeptical because of his size. Monte was a lot smaller than I thought you could be to be successful on the major college level. In the end, we took him. Thank God."

But Sloan also recruited one other point guard, Mark Moeller.

David Thompson, a college and NBA superstar who was Monte's teammate and roommate, remembers meeting Monte at NC State in the dorms just before school started in 1971:

"We were checking in at Sullivan Dorm, and some of the other guys were there. A guy named Joe Cafferky, he was a junior college transfer who wound up starting. He had this little guy with him. I thought he was his brother. He had cut off jeans and a tank top. I thought he was 14 years old. I didn't know who he was. When they told me who he was, I said, 'Man, we're going to be in trouble.'

"Later that evening, we played in some pickup games and his team always won. Right then, I found out Monte was a winner."

Regardless, Monte didn't begin his college career as a starter on the freshman team—at the time freshmen were ineligible to play varsity. Opportunity presented itself when the guard in front of him, Moeller, hurt his ankle in practice. Monte stepped in, the team went 15-1, and Sloan felt a lot better about his new point guard.

In their sophomore season, Monte, who averaged 10.0 points and 4.2 assists, and Thompson, a phenomenal 6-4 leaper who averaged 24.7 points and 8.1 rebounds, led NC State to a 27-0 record and No. 2 ranking in both the Associated Press and United Press International Polls. But there was no title to go with the undefeated season. The Wolfpack were on NCAA probation for recruiting infractions and were not allowed to participate in the Tournament. Fans were left to wonder how NC State might have fared against the team which did win the National Championship, UCLA.

Monte drives through the UCLA defense in the 1974 semi-finals of the
NCAA Tournament. It's known as one of the greatest games in college
basketball history. North Carolina State won in double overtime, 80-77.
Courtesy of Ken Hill, Sports Hotline
Photo by Robert Burke

The signature of the Wolfpack became the alley-oop pass, a lob near the rim for a great jumper to leap, catch the ball and score on an easy lay-in. Thompson's thunderous dunks off the alley-oop from Monte had to wait until their ABA and NBA careers. The NCAA had outlawed the dunk in 1967-68 and didn't reinstate it until 1976-77, two years after they left college.

It's a play which works only with perfect timing between two players: the right moment for the leaper to try to lose his man and rush to the basket, and the right instant for the passer to throw him the ball in a precise position over the rim. Monte and David Thompson did it as well as any.

"We practiced it, but after a while it was eye contact," Thompson said. "We played so much together, he knew when I'd go back door. He'd throw it up and I'd go get it. He was a great passer, the best passer I ever played with. He had a flair for the game."

And he wasn't a defensive liability as Sloan had feared: "What I was worried about was bigger guards taking him inside. We kept statistics on it. When they did it, it was very successful for us. They threw the ball away, or the shot was blocked by (7-foot-4 center Tommy) Burleson or Thompson."

The stranglehold UCLA held 20 years ago on college basketball was, is and always will be remarkable. The Bruins won 47 straight games from 1966-68, 41 straight from 1968-69, and an ungodly 88 in a row from 1971-74. UCLA won the national championship in 1964 and '65, and from 1967 through '73. Who could stop them in '74?

The Wolfpack tried and failed. In a nationally televised, early season showdown with the Bruins at a neutral site, St. Louis— with each team undefeated—UCLA, led by one of the greatest players in college basketball history, 6-11 center Bill Walton, won 84-66. The 18-point victory left no doubt that UCLA was still No. 1.

"Our motivation the rest of the year was to get into the NCAA Tournament to get another shot at them," Monte said.

Getting another chance at the Bruins wouldn't be easy. The NCAA Tournament field was 25 instead of today's 64, and there were no at-large bids for teams which failed to win their conference's automatic NCAA bid. That meant NC State had to win the post-season tournament of arguably the nation's toughest league at the time, the Atlantic Coast Conference (ACC).

Reaching the championship game led to a date with Maryland, laden with outstanding players John Lucas, Len Elmore, Tom McMillen and Mo Howard. "They were great and they were playing at a very high level," Monte said.

His team, too. NC State had won 31 consecutive ACC games and 52 of its last 53.

Maryland led by as many as 13 in the first half, but the Wolfpack rallied and sent the game into overtime. With six seconds left, and NC State up 101-100, Monte was fouled. He shot one and one: make the first free throw to get the chance to shoot the second. He made both. NC State won 103-100. Monte had 17 points and eight assists, and Thompson scored 29, but neither was the Wolfpack's leading scorer. That honor went to 7-4 center Tommy Burleson, who had been bypassed for the All-ACC center spot in favor of Elmore, who wound up with 18 points and 13 rebounds. Burleson matched Elmore's rebound total and scored 38 points. "Elmore said he deserved first team rather than me; that I wasn't fit to carry his shoes into the gym; that he had always been much better," said Burleson, who was named ACC Tournament MVP. "Coach Sloan taped that on my locker."

But the road to a UCLA rematch got only tougher, though the Wolfpack had the immense edge of playing the NCAA Eastern Regional at its own gym, Reynolds Coliseum. The Wolfpack beat a fourth-ranked Providence team led by All-American Marvin "Bad News" Barnes, 92-78, then trounced No. 8 Pittsburgh, 100-72, despite losing Thompson. In a frightening mid-air collision, Thompson caught the shoulder of a teammate and crashed to the floor, where he laid motionless. He was rushed to the hospital, but returned before the end of the game, receiving a tumultuous reception from the packed crowd of 12,400.

That set up the rematch with UCLA in the NCAA Semi-finals. "All during the week, nobody knew whether David was going to play," Monte said. "We had 6,000, 7,000 fans at practice."

Thompson would play and score 28 points in one of the most exciting games in college basketball history, one not resolved until double overtime. Monte played all 50 minutes and had 12 points and three assists, but Thompson values an even bigger contribution: "We were down seven in the second overtime. He came up with some big plays. He kept us fired up. He wouldn't let us quit."

There was exactly 2:07 left in the second overtime. UCLA had the ball out of bounds and a seven-point lead. Monte jumped in front of UCLA center Bill Walton, drew a charge, and made both ends of a one-and-one to cut the lead to five. The game's momentum turned. NC State won 80-77. Monte said, "We were going to win that game no matter what."

NC State won the National Championship two nights later, completing a 30-1 season by defeating Marquette, 76-64, with Monte scoring 16. Amid wild celebration, Monte went to the end of the NC State bench and simply sat down. "I wanted to take everything in," he said. "I remember a tremendous sense of satisfaction."

Actually, just minutes later, Sloan got a taste of how much pressure would be exerted on his newly-crowned champions: "One writer asked me immediately after the championship game, 'Is this the beginning of a new dynasty?' I said, 'That's ridiculous. That's ridiculous! We won one national championship. Let us enjoy it.'"

The Wolfpack had earned it: a remarkable 57-1 record over two seasons and the National Championship. Thompson, who averaged 26.0 points and 7.9 rebounds, was named Player of the Year, and Sloan Coach of the Year. Monte had averaged 12.8 points, 3.8 assists and 3.8 rebounds in his junior season.

With Burleson graduated, the Wolfpack slipped to 22-6 in Monte and David Thompson's senior year, losing the ACC Championship Game to North Carolina, 70-66. Monte averaged 10.4 points and 4.1 assists, and Thompson 29.9 points and 8.2 rebounds. "We were good, but we didn't live up to expectations," Monte said. "We missed Tommy tremendously. For my career, it was very important for me to play with Tommy. With my lack of size, it allowed me to gamble on defense. And on offense, Tommy was a real good passer who opened up things for everyone else."

Sloan mentioned another factor: "There was a lot of pressure on that ballclub. People just kept predicting big things, great things, an undefeated season. I think it just wore the players down. It got to be where it wasn't fun. The year before was fun."

Monte finished his career as NC State's all-time assist leader at 350, but the mark has been topped five times since by Chris Corchiani (1,038), Sidney Lowe (762), Clyde "The Glide" Austin (473), Nate McMillan (402) of the Seattle Supersonics, and Atlanta Hawks' Spud Webb (373).

The dimensions of professional basketball were changing rapidly when Thompson, voted two-time College Player of the Year by the Associated Press, and Monte finished their collegiate careers.

To the chagrin of the NBA, the rival American Basketball Association had not only survived since its inception in 1968, but was signing more big-name college seniors than the older, established league. The rift between the two leagues would finally be resolved after the 1976-77 season when four ABA teams: the Denver Nuggets, New York (now New Jersey) Nets, San Antonio Spurs and Indiana Pacers were absorbed into the NBA.

But the consolidation of the leagues was two years away when the Atlanta Hawks picked Thompson as the No. 1 selection of the 1975 NBA Draft. Monte was picked by the Hawks, too, in the fourth round. "It's a great thrill to be the first player picked," Thompson told reporters. "As to where my future lies, I have to wait until the ABA [Draft] and then weigh all matters as to what team or what league I'll be playing in."

The ABA's Denver Nuggets had the first pick in the 1975 Draft and chose center Marvin "The Human Eraser" Webster from Morgan State (Maryland). The Virginia Squires drafted Thompson No. 2. In the background, though, word came out that the Squires, who would eventually fold the next season, couldn't outbid the NBA's Hawks for Thompson's services.

Denver GM Carl Scheer thought he could.

Meanwhile, in the third round of the Draft, the Nuggets selected Monte. "I think they were in the recruiting business," Monte said. "They thought if they signed me, they'd have a better chance to sign David, but we never talked about it."

Scheer made the Squires an offer: All-Star guard Mack Calvin, starting forward Mike Green, and promising rookie Jan van Breda Kolff for the rights to Thompson. The Squires said "Yes," and Thompson and Monte were teammates again.

Together with the Nuggets, they'd play the final season of the ABA and Denver's first in the NBA. "It was a very exciting period to be with the Denver Nuggets," Monte said. "It was a fantastic experience. I was around great people, Larry Brown (coach), Carl Scheer (GM), Doug Moe, David Thompson, Dan Issel, Bobby Jones. It was a tremendous team we had in Denver."

The Nuggets went 60-24 in the last ABA season, losing in the Finals to Julius "Dr. J" Erving and the Nets, four games to two, then won the Midwest Division in their first NBA season, going 50-32. In the transition, though, Monte's playing time shrunk. "I played less minutes," he said. "The ABA game was more wide open, more up and down. The NBA was more big guards posting up. That didn't help players like myself. I felt, for the first time, my size really hurt me. Now, I was playing against the elite of the world."

Thompson, a prolific scorer whose number was retired by the Nuggets, was always glad to see Monte take the court: "We had a good running team. Pressure defense. We fast-breaked a lot. That fit in with the style Monte liked to play. I used to love it when he came in because he'd give me the alley-oop pass for a slam dunk. He'd get the crowd going. It was like the old days at NC State."

Not quite. In college, Monte was a vital starting player. In the pros, he wasn't.

In 1975-76, Monte averaged 3.0 points, 2.1 assists and exactly nine minutes in 64 games. In the NBA the following year, he appeared in 51 games, averaging 2.5 points, 1.7 assists and eight minutes. He shot exactly the same from the field (.406) in each season, and .818 and .720 from the foul line, respectively.

He was waived September 29, 1977. "I had a solid two years," he said. "I felt I contributed to two good basketball teams. I had run my course."

It didn't eliminate the pain. "It was not easy," he said. "Anytime, be it high school, college or pros, when they say you're not good enough, it's not easy to take. For some of us, it comes sooner. For others, it doesn't come at all. But in the NBA, those guys are the best in the world."

He stayed in Denver, doing TV and public relations work with the Nuggets before venturing into coaching, a profession he finds rewarding. "I enjoy what I'm doing," he said. "I never get tired of looking at film. I have a passion for basketball."

He was an assistant to Norm Sloan at North Carolina State from 1978-80, then with him at the University of Florida for 10 years.

"I always thought Monte would make a great coach," Sloan said. "He had a rapport with players as a player. I thought he'd maintain that rapport as a coach. He was a great

Monte with the Denver Nuggets.
Courtesy of Ken Hill, Sports Hotline
Photo by Ron McQueeney

recruiter. And he was all vim and vigor. I've played golf with Monte. I've played tennis with Monte. He's a fierce competitor. He just hates to lose. I thought he would pass that on to players and he did. He was just as effective as a coach as he was as a player."

Monte moved on to the Global Basketball Association as head coach at Raleigh and at Fayetteville, and then journeyed to Venezuela, where his team, Marinos de Oriente, went 31-11 in the 1992-93 regular season, then won the Professional Basketball League Championship, four to three in the seven-game finals.

"They were still partying when I left," he said. "The arena (in Puerto La Cruz) seats 5,500 and there was a sell-out every game the whole season. The enthusiasm for basketball is tremendous there. I'm guessing there was a minimum of 7,000 in the arena for the championship series. Fans would get there five hours before the game, buy general admission tickets and then sit inside the arena (the bleacher seats were first come, first serve). I really enjoyed my experience down there."

Not the second time around. He had signed a two-year contract, but two-thirds of the way into his second season, with his team 16-14, he was fired. "I was real disappointed," Monte said. "We had some injuries. We were just getting ready to play our best basketball of the season. If we could have gotten in the playoffs, I thought we had a chance to win it again."

Monte returned to America in the third week of April of 1994, and landed as an assistant to Flip Saunders with Sioux Falls in the CBA.

In the spring of 1995, he was named head coach of Chipola Junior College in Marianna, Florida. He's tried working as a television analyst in Denver and Charlotte, but his heart will always be in coaching. "Coaching is what I'm best at," he said. "Being an analyst is fun, but I want to be actively involved."

And just what would Monte the coach have thought of Monte the player? "I probably wouldn't have recruited that person," he said. "I didn't fit the ideal prototype."

Statistics

Monte Towe

Collegiate

Season	Team	G	Avg Pts	Avg Ast	Avg Reb	FG Pct	FT Pct	3 Pt Pct
1972-73	NC State	27	10.0	4.2	1.7	.468	.729	-
'73-74	NC State	31	12.8	3.8	3.8	.517	.811	-
'74-75	NC State	28	10.4	4.1	1.6	.469	.719	-

ABA

Season	Team	G	Avg Pts	Avg Ast	Avg Reb	Avg Stl	FG Pct	FT Pct	3 Pt Pct
1975-76	Denver	64	2.1	1.7	0.7	0.3	.406	.720	-

NBA

Season	Team	G	Avg Pts	Avg Ast	Avg Reb	Avg Stl	FG Pct	FT Pct	3 Pt Pct
1976-77	Denver	51	2.5	1.7	0.7	0.3	.406	.720	-

CHAPTER
6

Spud
5-7

He eyed the rim one more time, as if to see if it had moved, as if it could move. The chants continued:

"Spud! Spud! Spud!"

This was Dallas, his home.

This was the NBA Slam Dunk Contest, February 9, 1986.

This moment was his.

He tossed the ball high in the air in front of him and began his move to the basket. He waited for the ball to bounce and accelerated. Perfectly timing his jump, he intercepted the ball in one motion, cradled it in his hands the next, and slammed it through the net.

The crowd exploded. So did all the other players on hand for NBA All-Star Weekend. In one solitary moment, 5-foot-7 Anthony Jerome "Spud" Webb readjusted America's attitude toward small players. "I think it changed the way people looked at little guys," he said.

Spud shooting with the Atlanta Hawks.
Courtesy of the Atlanta Hawks

He was right. Even his teammates were stunned: "He'd never dunked [like that] in a game or in practice," guard Doc Rivers said. "We didn't know he could do it."

There was a reason. Spud, then a rookie with the Atlanta Hawks, has been dunking since the summer before his senior year in high school, but chose not to dunk in his new NBA environment. "I may have done one dunk in a game or practice," he said. "Nobody knew about the other dunks, but those were dunks I'd been doing for five years. I knew I had a repertoire of dunks. It was something natural that I could do. I was lucky they asked me to be in the contest."

His next NBA Coach, Garry St. Jean of Sacramento, remembered his reaction: "My jaw was down around my toes in amazement."

Spud won the Slam Dunk contest. But St. Jean isn't certain it didn't carry a price: "I don't think he's really gotten his due. He got recognized after the dunk achievement, but he's been a solid all-around performer."

For a decade. He has made a life in the NBA.

But he's never entered the Slam Dunk contest again. "I don't want to get into another one because people see you as a side show," he said. "I worked hard to get where I am. I want people to see me as a basketball player."

They do. "He's someone who's kind of shown what it takes to get the job done year in and year out," Alaa Abdelnaby, his former 6-10 teammate on the Sacramento Kings, said. "He has outstanding athletic ability. Certainly to be 5-7 and be able to take over a game, or dominate certain aspects of the game, is amazing itself."

Spud Webb is not still in the NBA because he can dunk a basketball. Rather, as the starting point guard, he was the architect of Sacramento's 39-43 season in '94-95, its best record in 11 years and a dramatic improvement from a dismal 28-54 record in 1993-94. The Kings reached mid-February at 28-21, and Spud won one of the games himself, hitting a short jump shot with 2.3 seconds left to give the Kings a 102-101 win against Portland, last December 27.

All Spud did was lead the NBA in foul shooting, while averaging 11.6 points and 6.2 assists.

"He brings it every night effort-wise," St. Jean said. "He's got a big heart just like all the small guys. He gets knocked around. If anything, it makes him more determined. He's got intense pride. He's a very determined guy who wants to be looked upon as a player who really gives it to you, who understands what winning is all about. I know the guys who play with him respect him. Other players around the league, too."

He's worked hard for it.

The second youngest of six children—three boys and three girls—he grew up in Dallas, where his father David works at a food market. Football, not basketball, was his passion—the Dallas Mavericks didn't join the NBA until 1980 when Spud was 16.

At a much earlier age, Spud was, and remains, a rabid Cowboys fan. "From Day One," he said, "I live and die with the Dallas Cowboys."

His heroes were Tony Dorsett, Roger Staubach and Drew Pearson, but he wasn't big enough to play professional football. And he was told many times he wasn't tall enough to play professional basketball. He just never paid attention.

His ties to Dallas, where his six-year-old daughter Lauren lives, remain strong. He annually hosts two charity events, the Spud Webb Basketball Weekend and a golf tournament, which benefit the Boys Club of Dallas. "I try to raise money for the kids," he said. "It keeps them out of trouble."

His nickname "Spud" was given to him as an infant not for a connection to a potato, but as short for the Russian satellite Sputnik. How could anyone have known he would someday be able to almost put himself in orbit with an astounding vertical leap of 42 inches?

He said he learned to dunk out of necessity: "Every guy around my high school could dunk. I was just trying to keep up with them."

He did, at 5-feet-4 as a senior in high school. Despite that, and despite the fact that he averaged 27 points a game at Wilmer-Hutchins High School in Dallas, no major college was interested in his services. No minor ones either.

"Nobody recruited me. Nobody," he said. "I was the smallest guy playing at the time. They didn't know if I could hold up in college. But the same guys who went on to Division I, I played against them in high school and in the summer."

With his options limited, he went to junior college at Midland (Texas), and led his team to the 1982 National Junior College Championship, picking up JUCO All-American honors along the way. He averaged 20.8 and 14.6 points in his two JUCO seasons, and Midland was 65-8.

Coach Jim Valvano offered Spud a scholarship to North Carolina State, and Spud didn't take long to make an impact. The 1983 Hall of Fame Tip-Off Classic in Springfield, Massachusetts, was a rematch of the 1983 National Championship game, when North Carolina State recorded one of the greatest upsets in the history of college basketball, beating Houston's Hakeem Olajuwon, Clyde Drexler and the rest of Phi Slamma Jamma, 54-52.

NC State won the rematch in Springfield, too, 76-64. Spud had 18 points, five assists, four rebounds and three steals. But Spud saved his first slam dunk for the home fans. In an 82-56 win over Hofstra, Spud put down two breakaway dunks.

The Wolfpack, though, didn't come close to repeating as national champions in Spud's first year. They finished 19-14, losing to Maryland, 69-63, in the first round of the ACC Tournament, then to Florida State, 74-71 in overtime, in the first round of the NIT. Spud averaged 9.8 points and 6.0 assists. He had 18 assists in a 77-74 win against Northeastern, which tied Sidney Lowe's NC State record set the season before. Chris Corchiani eclipsed both of them when he had 20 assists in a 114-91 win against Maryland, in 1991.

In Spud's senior season, 1984-85, NC State went 23-10, losing in the Finals of the NCAA West Regional to St. John's, 69-60. Spud averaged 11.1 points and 5.3 assists, identically matching his .761 free throw shooting from the year before. His 373 career assists in only two seasons still ranks No. 5 on NC State's all-time list.

He cherished his time at NC State because of the man he played for, Jim Valvano, who died from cancer in 1993 at the age of 47. "He was the type of coach you loved to play for, because he treated you like a man," Spud said.

Valvano was a man who took everything he could from life. "He'd tell stories, and come out and practice with us," Spud said. "He was an ideal coach."

The Detroit Pistons made Spud the 87th player taken overall in the 1985 draft when they selected him in the fourth round. He's still not sure why: the Pistons released him before training camp started, September 24, 1985. "They drafted me, but they never gave me a chance," he said.

He had a back-up plan. The Atlanta Hawks had expressed interest in his services. Atlanta signed him as a free agent just two days after Detroit released him.

Seven-foot-1 Tree Rollins, now an assistant coach/player with the Orlando Magic, was a teammate of Charlie Criss and Spud in Atlanta. "The first day I met Spud, he'd just gotten cut by Detroit," Tree said. "Mike Fratello was our coach. We were down in Charleston, South Carolina, at training camp. This little guy shows up. He's having a decent camp the first couple of days. Then in our morning workout, he caught an elbow in his mouth. It ripped out some of his teeth. He went to the dentist and came back to evening practice ready to go. I guess he figured he had to go back. I called Mike to the side. I said we got to keep him. You can't replace a guy with a heart his size. Even to today, I call him my idol."

Despite the dental work—Fratello didn't let him practice that night—getting cut by the Pistons may have been the best thing possible for Spud's career. In Detroit, he wouldn't have seen much playing time behind all-time great Isiah Thomas, NBA All-Star Joe Dumars and super sub Vinnie "Microwave" Johnson. In Atlanta, Spud found his niche, appearing in 79 of 82 games his rookie season, averaging 7.8 points and 4.3 assists, excellent numbers because he was only playing 15.6 minutes a night.

His defining moment was in the 1986 Slam Dunk Contest, but the fact is that he built his career throughout that solid season. In his second NBA start two weeks after the Slam Dunk, he scored 23 points and had 13 assists against the Lakers.

Thus began Spud's dilemma. He had stunned the world by winning the Slam Dunk Contest, but he had no intention of relying on a gimmick to shape his career. He wanted to play every game, and he wanted to start every game. "I've always said I was good enough to be a full-time player," he said.

His agent, Robin Blakely, put it this way: "The rest of the world may see Spud as a role player, but Spud believes he is good enough to start in the NBA. You can tell him that's not so, and he may not get his chance, but that will never dissuade him. And if Spud didn't think that way, I don't think he could play in the league as small as he is."

Spud's second season was a bust. Leg injuries limited him to 33 games, though his numbers were okay: 6.8 points and 5.1 assists.

Spud went on to play four more seasons with the Hawks, appearing in 320 of a possible 328 games. He accomplished this despite the physical punishment every player routinely receives in the NBA.

In a string of games in February 1991, he got knocked to the floor by Chicago's Horace Grant one night, then belted by the Nets' Jack Haley, and then sent headfirst into the basket support by Seattle's Shawn Kemp. "It's the nature of the game," Spud said at the time. "You're playing well, they want to stop you, so they foul you."

Spud on the move.
Courtesy of the Atlanta Hawks

Spud's best two seasons in Atlanta were his last two. In '89-90, he averaged 9.2 points and 5.8 assists.

His '90-91 season began with him on the bench. But Coach Bob Weiss, who saw his Hawks struggle—they were on their way to losing nine in a row early in the season—put Spud into the starting line-up at the end of November. Spud doubled his production from the bench, 6.6 points and 3.1 assists, to 12.8 and 6.4, respectively, and the Hawks went 30-15 through the middle of the season. Spud finished the season averaging 13.4 points and 5.6 assists, but the Hawks traded him, along with a 1994 second round draft pick, to Sacramento for Travis Mays, a 6-2 guard, on July 1, 1991.

"Nobody wants to get traded," Spud said. "You play in one place for a long time...Atlanta was a great city. They were great guys. It was hard. But I was going to get an opportunity for myself. You see a trade as bad at first, but it's better to get traded than cut. At least somebody wants you."

Mays wound up playing two games for the Hawks in the entire '91-92 season, though he averaged 7.0 points in 49 games the following year.

Spud remains among the Hawks' Top Ten in career free throw percentage (fourth), three-pointers made (seventh), assists (eighth) and steals (ninth). He's also third in three-pointers attempted.

But he prospered in California.

His career highs in points, assists and rebounds have all come with the Kings. He had 34 points against Golden State, April 21, 1993, and scored 32 three other times with the Kings—he also had 32 once with the Hawks. His top assist mark of 17 came against the Clippers, March 23, 1993. He somehow managed to get nine rebounds twice, against Indiana and Dallas, on April 17, 1993, and November 29, 1993.

In his first three seasons in Sacramento, he averaged 16.0, 14.5 and 12.7 points and 7.1, 6.9 and 6.7 assists. In 1993-94, he ranked 12th in the NBA in assists, 34th in free throw percentage (.813) and 38th in three-point percentage (.335).

Spud with the Sacramento Kings.
Courtesy of the Sacramento Kings

Regardless of the decent, if unspectacular numbers, and although he signed a four-year contract extension with the Kings during the 1991-92 season, Spud was rumored to be traded by the Kings many times. In the summer of '93, published reports said both the San Antonio Spurs and the New Jersey Nets had shown interest in obtaining him.

Late in July 1994, Spud thought for sure he was gone, in a trade to the Orlando Magic for point guard Scott Skiles. "People were calling me up and telling me it was done," he said.

But instead, the Magic traded Skiles, a 1996 first round draft pick and future considerations to the Washington Bullets for a 1996 second round draft pick and future considerations. In dealing Skiles, the Magic opened up his $2.05 million salary slot, which allowed them to sign free agent forward Horace Grant of the Chicago Bulls.

Spud was shocked his deal didn't materialize. "Right up from under my feet," he said. "I was afraid to say anything before the trade was done because I was afraid something like this was going to happen. But I had been told the deal was practically done.

"The trade didn't surprise me because the Kings have been trying to trade me for two years. I wish it would have gone through. I was getting excited about playing for a championship-type team."

Instead, he remained with the Kings. "I soured on the game the past couple of years," he said. "But you know what your job is and you try to be loyal to your teammates. Not to your team, because if they don't show loyalty to you, it's tough to be loyal to them. It's tough, because you know the team doesn't want you."

Yet he had a great 1994-95 season, one which ended with disappointment. The Kings lost a chance for their first playoff appearance since 1986 when they lost their final game at Denver.

Winning with disgruntled players had been accomplished before—big time. The Houston Rockets traded forward

Spud with the Sacramento Kings.
Courtesy of the Sacramento Kings
Photo by Rocky Widner

Robert Horry, Matt Bullard and two future second-round draft picks to the Detroit Pistons for Sean Elliott, February 4, 1994. Elliott failed a physical; the trade was voided, February 7, and Horry returned to Houston to help the Rockets win two consecutive NBA championships.

Nobody predicted the same scenario for Spud and the Kings in 1994-95, but Spud enjoyed the Kings' unprecedented success. "The franchise was down," he said last season. "We just didn't have the personnel to compete every night. I'm kind of happy that I'm here since we turned it around. I feel like I'm a part of it."

He was, until June 29, 1995, when the Kings, who selected national collegiate champion UCLA's point guard Tyus Edney the night before in the NBA draft, traded Spud back to Atlanta for veteran forward Tyrone Corbin.

The Kings finally did give up on Spud, who is only 31. "My agent told me once that when a point guard starts to go, free throws are the first thing to go," he said.

If that's true, Spud is headed in the opposite direction. He's always been a good foul shooter, checking in at .835 in his first nine seasons. In his 10th, he led the NBA at .934, making 226 of 242 free throws. Cleveland's Mark Price was second (.914), Dana Barros of Philadelphia third (.899), Indiana's Reggie Miller fourth (.897), and Muggsy Bogues fifth (.889).

"Foul shooting is just concentration," Spud said. "I play golf and putting is like a free throw."

Actually, golf to him is like an addiction. "In the summer, I get a tee time the first thing when I get up, if I don't have the time set from the night before," he said. Though he claims to be "terrible" with a 15 handicap, he said, "I can keep up."

He's already taken his daughter golfing, "She's got a nice swing," he said.

He may have to work some to keep her from getting as competitive on the golf course as her dad. "I hate to lose playing anything," he said.

He's still winning on the basketball court by playing his kind of game. "I don't try to go out and score 50 a game," he said. "I play team basketball. I try to come to play every night, and I don't back down to anybody."

Sacramento Coach Garry St. Jean remains one of Spud's biggest fans: "He gave us an advantage because he's a fighter. It never hurts to have people who really want to work hard and win. Talent in this league is a given. What really cuts players apart from each other is their focus and determination. He's achieved his maximum."

Statistics

Spud Webb

Collegiate

Season	Team	G	Avg Pts	Avg Ast	Avg Reb	FG Pct	FT Pct	3 Pt Pct
1981-82	Midland	38	20.8	7.1	2.0	.515	.781	-
'82-83	Midland	35	14.6	10.1	3.0	.445	.774	-
'83-84	NC State	33	9.8	6.0	1.8	.459	.761	-
'84-85	NC State	33	11.1	5.3	2.0	.481	.761	-

NBA

State	Team	G	Avg Pts	Avg Ast	Avg Reb	Avg Stl	FG Pct	FT Pct	3 Pt Pct
1985-86	Atlanta	79	7.8	4.3	1.6	1.0	.483	.785	.182
'86-87	Atlanta	33	6.8	5.1	1.8	1.0	.438	.762	.167
'87-88	Atlanta	82	6.0	4.1	1.8	0.8	.475	.817	.053
'88-89	Atlanta	81	3.9	3.5	1.5	0.9	.459	.867	.045
'89-90	Atlanta	82	9.2	5.8	2.5	1.3	.477	.871	.053
'90-91	Atlanta	75	13.4	5.6	2.3	1.6	.447	.868	.321
'91-92	Sacramento	77	16.0	7.1	2.9	1.6	.445	.859	.367
'92-93	Sacramento	69	14.5	7.0	2.8	1.5	.433	.851	.274
'93-94	Sacramento	79	12.7	6.7	2.8	1.2	.460	.813	.335
'94-95	Sacramento	76	11.6	6.2	2.3	1.0	.438	.934	.302

Charlie
5-8

What is faith? How many years can it survive?

   "I always believed I would play in the NBA," Charlie Criss said. "Other people told me I wouldn't make it, but that kept me going. It motivated me to show them they were wrong, and they sure were."

Coaches, parents, everybody. But it took so long for him to prove it, so long that he became an NBA rookie at the ancient age of 28. He may be the NBA's oldest rookie ever—he is certainly one of the oldest.

Once he made it, he stuck in the NBA for eight seasons.

Once he made it, he got a letter from Ed Murphy, who had been the assistant coach of his college team, New Mexico State. "He had said I'd never make it in the NBA, that I was too small," Charlie said. "He sent me a letter 10 years later apologizing. He thought they weren't going to take small guys. At that time they weren't."

Charlie forced their hand. He refused to quit on himself, even when he failed to make the roster of a team in the minor Eastern League—which became the Continental Basketball Association (CBA)—and he pried his way into the most exclusive pool of basketball talent in the world.

It wasn't easy, and there certainly weren't any shortcuts.

He was born in Valhalla, New York, 20 miles from Yonkers, the oldest of 11 children of Charles Sr. and his wife Mildred. There is no similarity to the classic tale of a playground legend wowing scouts since he first began playing. The fact is, Charlie didn't play basketball until he was in the eighth grade. And when he did, he was terrible.

"I'd never picked up a basketball," he said. "It had nothing to do with height. We just played handball and stickball." (He'd played shortstop in baseball in high school.)

When he was in the fourth grade, his family moved to California for eight months but returned to Greenburgh, a suburb of White Plains. They then moved to Yonkers, where Charles Sr. worked as a chef at Howard Johnson's and as a pin-setter at a bowling alley to raise his enormous family. "He just did what he had to do," Charlie said. "He said, 'Do what you had to do in order to survive. Just keep going.'"

Charlie learned and lived that work ethic.

His motivation to play basketball sprang from peer pressure. His buddies were trying out for the junior high (grades 7-9) team. So he did, too, unsuccessfully. "Of course I didn't make the team because I couldn't play," he said. "I threw a layup over the backboard."

When he was cut, he told the coach, Joe Flower, he'd be back next year. The coach laughed in his face.

Though he might not have needed more motivation than that, he received it when he got home that day. "I told my mother and father I was going to play basketball, and they both laughed at me," Charlie said. "That motivated me. I made up my mind I wanted to play and I just stayed with it. I just got good."

His mom remembered the moment: "We thought it was a joke when he said he wanted to play basketball. We thought he was too short at first. But he was very determined. He was determined not to let anyone stop him. I'm very proud of him."

Once Charlie discovered basketball, he didn't stop playing. Do the dishes and run to the playground. Clean up the house and run outside. The weather didn't matter: "Once I started playing, I played seven days a week, rain or shine. It made no difference. We shoveled snow off the court. Any time my mom or father wanted to find me, they knew where I was.

"I didn't want to be an average player. I wanted to play professionally. It was in my blood. I used to watch Oscar Robertson, John Havlicek and Jerry West. I really admired them. That was what I wanted to do. I was going to do it, or die trying."

He had unexpected help learning the game. Ed Foley, a former college player, had two sons who had gone to Yonkers High School. Charlie would play there through his junior year before transferring to nearby Gorton High School after his family moved following a fire in their apartment building. Nobody was home at the time and there were no injuries.

"Ed Foley had a two-hand set shot," Charlie said. "He just happened to be at the park when I went to play one day. I said I was learning how to play. He said, 'I can help you.' He did. He sure did. He helped me with my fundamentals, dribbling, passing, shooting. He worked with me every day for the whole summer. He was good. He just knew the game. Everything he knew, he taught me."

Then Charlie's talents burst out. He was quick, an excellent ballhandler and a deft outside shooter. In the ninth grade, he was the best player on the junior high team.

In the 10th grade, he got called up to the varsity, but played infrequently. He handled that: "It didn't really bother me that much. I was up there for the experience."

When he transferred to Gorton High School for his senior year, his career exploded skyward. He was almost his full height of 5-8 when he began lighting up scoreboards around Westchester County. "Everything took off," he said.

He made All-City (Yonkers) and All-County, averaging 25 points a game on Gorton's 19-2 team, and he was recruited heavily. Among the some 50 teams interested were Manhattan, Villanova, Iona (New York), University of Texas-El Paso (UTEP), Pepperdine, Corpus Christi and New Mexico State.

New Mexico State Coach Lou Henson—now the coach at the University of Illinois—remembers recruiting Charlie: "We called his high school coach, John Volpe. He said, 'If you're going to bring a measuring stick, don't even bother. But if you want a top player, come and get him.'"

He did, as Charlie decided to play across the country: "I guess I just wanted to get away from New York," he said.

Soon afterwards, he wanted to get back.

In his freshman season, New Mexico State didn't have any scholarships left, and farmed him out to New Mexico Junior College. "They asked me if I'd do that, and I said, 'Yes,'" he said. He was the fifth leading junior college scorer in the country (32 points a game), and he was named a JUCO All-American.

He expected a smooth transition to New Mexico State the following season as a sophomore, but instead wound up as a back-up on the Aggies' bench. So he left before the Christmas break. This man who would conquer years and years of challenges went home. "I was mad because I wasn't starting," he said. "I was playing behind a guy named Paul Landis, a senior. I thought I should have been starting."

Right about then, his career could have expired. Fortunately for him, New Mexico State Assistant Coach Ed Murphy flew to New York after the season, and convinced him to return to college. He started as a junior and averaged 16.7 points and 5.0 assists as a junior. One of his teammates was 6-10 junior center Sam Lacey, who would go on to play in the NBA for 13 seasons.

But it was Charlie who made the Aggies go. "Charlie Criss was a tremendous ballplayer," Henson said. "He has a lot of will power. He's very intelligent, very intense. When he does something, he goes all the way."

He kicked off his junior season in style, being named MVP of the Dedication Tournament, held to honor the Aggies' new $3.5 million Pan American Center. Charlie scored 31 against Colorado State in the opener and 19 against UTEP in the final.

He scored 32 against Hardin Simmons in a 74-68 road win in Abilene, Texas, and 25 against Tennessee Tech and Arizona State as the Aggies raced to a 12-0 record. They reached 15-1 and finished 24-5.

With their entire line-up back the following season, the Aggies were set to make a run for the national championship. But it was a voyage which started without Charlie. In a scrimmage before his senior season, he landed badly coming down with a rebound and broke the metatarsal bone in his right foot. He missed several games, but returned to lead New Mexico State to the 1970 NCAA Final Four. The Aggies were beaten in the semifinals by eventual champion UCLA—featuring Sidney Wicks and Curtis Rowe—then won third place by beating St. Bonaventure in the consolation to finish 27-3.

Charlie wasn't pleased with his performance that season, though he averaged 12.5 points on a Final Four team: "I played okay, but to me, I didn't play that well."

A majority opinion. He wasn't drafted. The Utah Stars in the ABA invited him to a tryout camp. He thought he played well, but was cut. "They never said why," he said. "They just cut me."

He returned to Las Cruces, taking a job as a collection officer in a bank and playing AAU ball for two years around the state. "I wanted to stay in New Mexico and try to get my foot completely healthy," he said. "The doctor said my foot wouldn't heal until I rested it and stopped playing on it. But I never gave up on my goal. I just knew I could play."

Charlie takes charge for New Mexico State.
Courtesy of New Mexico State

He returned to New York two years later. "It was time to go," he said. "I was ready to give it a shot."

But there was no magic when he began playing in recreation leagues and on the playgrounds around Yonkers again. No super discovery story on his first day back, or his first week back or first month or first year. Or two years. Or three.

He lived in an apartment in Yonkers and worked at Tuck Tape Manufacturing in nearby New Rochelle doing data processing in the accounting department for four years. And he played.

"I just wanted to get a chance to play in the NBA," he said. "All I wanted was an opportunity. The only way I could get it was with the Eastern League."

He got cut there, too, after trying out with the Hartford Capitols in 1972. "They had a guy named Eddie Griffith at point guard," Charlie said. "He had been there a long time. The coach, Pete Monska, didn't believe in small players. The next year, I came back. I beat out Eddie Griffith even though it was the same coach."

In the interim, he got the break he desperately wanted, a thin window of opportunity for a guy who was told his entire life he was neither good enough nor tall enough to make it to the NBA.

After being cut by Hartford, he played with a neighborhood team out of the Runyon Heights Community Center. In an Easter Tournament in Yonkers, he had the fortune of playing against the Courtsmen, a team which played in the Harlem Pro League, a summer haven for NBA and college stars and wanna-be stars. Charlie played well against the Courtsmen, and after the game, their coach, Teddy Jones, asked Charlie to join their team.

He did. He began playing everywhere he possibly could, finally getting opportunities to be seen. In the Harlem Pro League, he got to test his skills against Dr. J., Tiny Archibald, Billy Paultz, World B. (Lloyd) Free, Henry Bibby and other NBA name players. He also played in Philadelphia's Baker

League against NBA caliber players. But again in his life, there was no shortcut, only a long road measured in years.

In 1975, his college coach Lou Henson offered him advice: "I told him, 'You've been trying for years. You're not going to make it in the NBA. You need to do something else and get on with your life.'"

Uh-uh. "Charlie had that burning desire," Henson said. "He showed me that he could make it."

Charlie returned to the weekends-only Eastern League, and was twice named the league's MVP, in '75-76 and '76-77. He led the Hartford Capitols to the 1973-74 title and the Scranton Apollos to the championship three years later. In between, he also played with Cherry Hill (New Jersey), with his old coach Pete Monska. He was the Eastern League's leading scorer three consecutive years.

Horror stories of playing and traveling conditions and/or lack of paychecks populate the Eastern League's history then, but not for Charlie: "It wasn't that bad. With Hartford, I made about $50 a game. With Scranton about $80. You had to drive on your own to get to places, but it was great basketball. It was the next best thing to being in the pros."

He wasn't about to give up. "One night I scored 72 points in the Eastern League and another I had 63 with Hartford," he said. "But when I found I could go by guys like Nate Archibald, Henry Bibby and World B. Free in those summer leagues, I didn't need anybody to tell me I could play in the NBA. What I needed was a chance."

And he got one, only to fail. After his '75-76 MVP season, he was invited to the camp of the New York Knicks. He lasted until the day before the 1976-77 exhibition season started when he was cut. Six-foot-1 free agent Dennis "Mo" Layton and Jim Barnett, who was later waived without playing a game in the regular season, beat him out. "I didn't handle it real well because I couldn't understand it," Charlie said. "I thought I at least would get a chance to play exhibition games and be seen by other teams."

So he returned to the Eastern League and had his second MVP season. That summer of '77, he spent two and a half months touring Europe with the Washington Generals, the team which accompanies and almost always loses to the Harlem Globetrotters, while intermittently playing their foils in on-court pranks. "I didn't play in most of the funny quarters," he said. "I played in the quarters we played straight. I didn't like looking like a fool. I loved basketball too much."

Charlie got to see London; Rome, Naples and Bologna, Italy; Munich, Germany; Barcelona and Madrid, Spain; Sweden and Denmark. "It was fun. It was very exciting," he said. "I'd never been out of the country."

When he returned to the U.S., he had a message from his agent, Steve Kauffman. The Atlanta Hawks had invited him to their 1977-78 pre-season camp. "I asked Steve, 'Are they legit, or do they want a practice player?'"

Kauffman told him that Hawks scout Hal Wissel had been very impressed with Charlie in the Eastern League. Wissel, now with the Milwaukee Bucks, in turn gave Hawks Coach Hubie Brown a hard-sell. "Somebody asked Hal, 'He's only 5-8. Who can he guard?'" Hubie said. "Hal told them, 'Who can guard him?'"

After inheriting a team which went 29-53, Brown guided the Hawks to a 31-51 record in his first season, 1976-77. In January of '77, Ted Turner bought the Hawks. "He bought the team and cut the budget, and I made a decision that what we were going to do is press and trap for 48 minutes," Hubie said. "So we were only going to keep four players from the previous season. We were opening it up to eight other guys. The guards had to be quick and good foul shooters and be able to take his man to the basket. The main thing I wanted was the best guys available from the Eastern League."

Charlie Criss fit the bill. "Hal came to me with so much glowing description of his quickness and his ability to push the ball from circle to circle," Hubie said. Hubie also liked

Charlie's scoring average and field goal percentage and especially his high foul shooting percentage, because teams that
fast break continually will get more trips to the foul line.

To get Charlie to camp—he still wanted to try out for the
Knicks "just to be in New York" he said—Hubie guaranteed
he'd get to play in all eight exhibition games. "I didn't want
the same thing to happen that did the year before," Charlie
said. "I wanted a real chance and he agreed to it. And they
gave me a $1,000 bonus."

If this was going to be his final shot at the NBA, all he
wanted was to play enough minutes to prove he belonged, to
make an NBA roster, and then see what happened.

Training camp was extremely difficult for him. For open-
ers, he was 28, six or seven years older than other rookies in
camp fresh out of college. Secondly, from playing in the run
and gun Eastern League, he was unaccustomed to disciplined
offense and pressing defense. Thirdly, he had to contend with
the other Hawks guards, rookie Eddie Johnson from Auburn
and two second-year players, Armond Hill and Ken Charles.
All four guards would make the team.

"Charlie didn't get credit for being a 28-year-old-rookie,"
Hubie said. "He struggled in camp."

But Hubie, as well as Assistant Coach Frank Layden—the
former coach and now president of the Utah Jazz—quickly
fell in love with him. "Everybody loved him," Layden said.
"Charlie Criss is one of the most wonderful persons I've ever
known. He came up the hard way. He was tough as nails, an
overachiever. Everybody loved him. He was old fashioned.
He knew how to pass; he knew how to shoot. A tough guy.
He had to be. Everybody said he was a great summer player,
a great CBA player. Hubie said he was our kind of player. To
be the quarterback for us, you had to be somebody special."

Hubie found a lot to like about his 28-year-old rookie: "He
was extremely likeable, very coachable, and a very, very hard
worker. The only two players who I ever coached in the pros
in 14 years that I thought really enjoyed playing were Eddie

Johnson and Charlie Criss. They played one on one a half hour before practice; practiced for two hours, and played one on one half an hour after practice. They were always working on their game. You can't be Charlie's size and excel at the NBA level without having a great heart, because, not only does it take incredible physical discipline, but also the mental discipline. The game is so demanding when you are that size."

By sheer coincidence, Charlie's first NBA game was on the road at Madison Square Garden against the New York Knicks. "It was great; it was fantastic," he said. "Every night I hit the floor, I said, 'I was in the NBA.'"

In the Hawks' second game, on the road against the Boston Celtics, Charlie scored 21. The game was played at the Celtics' New England home away from home, Hartford, Connecticut, where Charlie had toiled in the Eastern League.

Funny thing. Not only could Charlie play in the NBA, but true to Hubie Brown's words, he did excel. A man once rejected by the Eastern League finished as the Atlanta Hawks' third leading scorer with an 11.4 average, almost entirely as a reserve and despite a jammed sore thumb on his (right) shooting hand that bothered him for a couple months. More significantly, the Hawks improved with him on the court, jumping up 10 wins from the previous season to 41-41, as Hubie Brown was named Coach of the Year. The Hawks made the playoffs for the first time in five seasons, and they would improve even more to 46-36 and 50-31 the following two years.

"Charlie was a prime-time scorer," Hubie said. "His range was outstanding. He was great off the dribble, and could score in traffic. He and Calvin Murphy could shoot with either hand, and they could stop on a dime. You had to honor their range, and then they would beat you off the dribble because of their outstanding explosion and quickness. Charlie would stop and fade back and shoot it over seven-foot people. And you could never foul Charlie because he was a mid-80 percent foul shooter."

Charlie drives to the hoop.
Courtesy of the Atlanta Hawks

Perhaps most surprising was that despite popular opinion, Charlie was not a defensive liability because of his size. This was partially true because the Hawks would constantly mix full-court, three-quarter court and half-court presses, frequently putting two players on whoever had the ball. "Because we pressed and trapped, we could hide people," Hubie said. "Size was not a criteria because Charlie was never in the same place on the court."

When teams tried to freeze him in one place—in the low post against inevitably much taller guards—the Hawks would double team the post or double team the dribbler. Charlie would front the post player and rely on weak-side help. "The rules for illegal zone defenses were much less strict then, so we could always help," Hubie said. "We were never concerned about him defensively, because of the way we played."

But the joy of Charlie's rookie season was tempered by the death of his father in December. Charles Sr. had listened to Charlie's NBA games on the radio, but tragically never got to see him in an NBA game.

"At the funeral, I got sick. I just started having bad cramps in my stomach," Charlie said. "They found out that because of the stress of the funeral, I had ileitis colitis."

His mother was deeply concerned: "I was afraid he'd stop playing after his father died. He was so depressed. But he never gave up. He decided to play not only for himself, but for his father, too."

Charlie stayed in the hospital a week, and then met the team for a game in Phoenix, January 17. "I was so tired at the game," Charlie said. "I hadn't played. Hubie played me. I got hot shooting. I motioned him to take me out. He wouldn't. He just said slow it up." Charlie scored a then career high 30, 22 in the fourth quarter, in a 103-101 loss.

Charlie appeared in 77 of 82 games his rookie season, averaging a considerable 25.1 minutes. Besides his 11.4 scoring average, he averaged 3.7 assists, 1.6 rebounds and

1.4 steals. He shot .425 from the field, .797 at the line and even blocked five shots.

His closest friend on the Hawks was another of the Hawks' four rookies, 7-foot-1 Wayne "Tree" Rollins, now an assistant coach/player with the Orlando Magic. "Charlie and I hit it off pretty good," said Tree, who is six years Charlie's junior. "We were Mutt and Jeff. I had never really played with a guy that small and a guy that quick to get his shot off. It was amazing the things he could do."

It was amazing what they both did as rookies. Back then, being a rookie meant catering to the veterans. "We had to do all the grunt work, so we got pretty close," Tree said. "We had to carry the shot clocks with us for exhibition games. The rookies were the bellmen for the team. We delivered their bags, delivered their uniforms. We'd always go out together and hide out from the veterans. We were always taking in movies together. We'd just hang out together in our apartment complex. Today, the rookies really don't have to do anything. It's too easy to play now."

Tree, who played his high school ball in Georgia, and his college ball in South Carolina at Clemson University, grew fond of the little guy from Yonkers, New York. "He was a typical New Yorker," Tree said. "He was cocky and very strong minded. Nothing could stand in his way. He was a hard worker."

With that hard work, he proved a lot of people wrong. One was Bob Kauffman, who scouted Charlie in the Eastern League as the Hawks assistant general manager before moving on to be head coach and GM of the Detroit Pistons in the middle of the '77-78 season. "I didn't think he could make it," Kauffman said in a newspaper interview midway through Charlie's rookie season. "But Charlie is sticking that right in my ear. I was wrong. He can play. But he couldn't play for just any team in the NBA. Atlanta is a disciplined team, and he's a disciplined player."

A smiling Charlie could play in the NBA after all.
Courtesy of the Atlanta Hawks

Somewhere along the line, Charlie's nickname "Mosquito" (from the Harlem Pro League) became "Bam Bam." "Skip Caray of TBS gave me that because I was so strong in my upper body," Charlie said. "They did all the Hawks games." Charlie would, too.

In '78-79, he appeared in 54 games—he had to have surgery on a separated shoulder—averaging 5.3 points and 2.6 assists in 16.3 minutes a night. The following year, he appeared in 81 games, averaging 22.1 minutes, 8.3 points and 3.0 assists.

A sprained left ankle allowed him to play in only 66 games in '80-81, but he finished seventh in the NBA in free throw percentage (.864). Larry Bird (.863) was eighth. Charlie averaged 25.8 minutes, 9.5 points and 4.6 assists. He scored a season-high 21 points against both the Nets and the Knicks.

But Hubie Brown was fired as coach with three games left in the 1980-81 season, and Kevin Loughery, who would later coach the Chicago Bulls, Washington Bullets and Miami Heat, took over that summer.

Charlie was averaging 20.4 minutes and 8.7 points in '81-82, but when Eddie Johnson and Wes Matthews returned from injuries, his role diminished. After 27 games with the Hawks, Charlie was traded with Al Wood to the San Diego (now Los Angeles) Clippers for Freeman Williams, January 20, 1982.

Charlie scored a career high 34 for the Clippers against San Antonio before he broke his jaw when he caught an inadvertent elbow in the face from Phil Ford of the Kings. He missed the final two months of the '81-82 season. He'd averaged 12.9 points and 4.0 assists in 28 games with the Clippers, shooting .479 from the field and .884 at the foul line. For the entire season, his free throw percentage of .887 was second in the NBA, behind only Kyle Macy of Phoenix at .899.

Yet Charlie had done anything but found a home. The Clippers released him, and the Milwaukee Bucks signed him as a free agent, September 30, 1982.

Charlie played in 66 games with the Bucks in '82-83, averaging 6.2 points and 1.9 assists.

He got in six games with Milwaukee the following season before being waived, November 23, 1983. Charlie rejoined the Hawks as a television analyst with TBS for the first of four seasons, but had two more brief flings playing for them. Later in the '83-84 season, Atlanta signed him to a 10-day contract, and he played in nine games.

In '84-85, he came off the TV sidelines for another 10-day contract with the Hawks, playing four games.

He remains seventh (.823) on the all-time Hawks' list of career free throw percentage leaders.

While also working as a substitute teacher (grade school and high school) in Atlanta, he currently works as a golf instructor. "I started playing golf when I stopped playing basketball 10 years ago," he said. "It came to me pretty quickly."

Coaching didn't. He got his first chance to coach professionally, April 29, 1991, when he was named head coach of the first-year Atlanta Eagles in the summer United States Basketball League. Previously, he'd only coached in recreational leagues and pro-am exhibition games.

He learned of the job because his wife, Mary, noticed a newspaper article about the new team being organized. "I just called the guy up and had an interview with him," Charlie said.

The "guy" was Eagles' President and General Manager Charlie Pecchio. "Charlie [Criss] has always proven that he likes to win," Pecchio said that season. "He works well with players and knows them. We see the game the same way, and I think that's important. I felt real comfortable that I could work with him."

The Eagles went 10-10. Two of his players were longtime friend World B. Free, one of the greatest scoring guards in NBA history, and his former teammate on the Hawks, Wes Matthews. Most of the players in the USBL had much lower profiles. "They were young guys trying to make it to the NBA," Charlie said. "They just didn't get paid like NBA players."

He could relate to that. Actually, the Eagles were paid $300 a game for the two-month season.

"It was fun," Charlie said. "It was the start of a new team. We had almost 200 players try out over two weekends."

After the season, the team was sold, and the new owners didn't keep Charlie as coach.

He remains in Atlanta with his wife, Mary, their three children, Chas, Tina and Edwin, two children by his first wife, Alisia and Theresa, and one of his seven grandchildren, Alexandria, now three. He has a 2 handicap in golf.

Some thought he had a handicap in basketball, but they were wrong.

Statistics

Charlie Criss

Collegiate

Season	Team	G	Avg Pts	Avg Ast	Avg Reb	FG Pct	FT Pct	3 Pt Pct
1967-68	New Mex St.	11	7.3	0.6	1.2	.410	.741	-
'68-69	New Mex St.	26	16.7	2.2	3.0	.460	.794	-
'69-70	New Mex St.	24	12.5	2.9	2.3	.398	.398	-

NBA

Season	Team	G	Avg Pts	Avg Ast	Avg Reb	Avg Stl	FG Pct	FT Pct	3 Pt Pct
1977-78	Atlanta	77	11.4	3.8	1.6	1.4	.425	.797	-
'78-79	Atlanta	54	5.3	2.6	1.1	0.8	.377	.779	-
'79-80	Atlanta	81	8.3	3.0	1.4	0.9	.431	.811	.059
'80-81	Atlanta	66	9.5	4.3	1.5	0.9	.454	.864	.048
'81-82	Atl/S. Diego	56	10.8	3.4	1.5	0.8	.446	.887	.345
'82-83	Milwaukee	66	6.2	1.9	1.2	0.4	.451	.895	.194
'83-84	Milw/Atlan	15	3.5	2.5	1.3	0.5	.385	.750	.167
'84-'85	Atlanta	4	4.5	5.5	3.5	0.8	.412	.667	.000

Murray
5-9

When Murray Wier led the nation in scoring in 1947-48 at the University of Iowa, the Big Ten was only the Big Nine. That may make him sound outdated, but, in fact, he was a player way ahead of his time. He was a one-hand shooter when just about everybody else in the basketball universe shot with two. He shot on the run; others got set first. His sky hook—conceived out of necessity against taller opponents—preceded Kareem's by three decades. Above all, Murray Wier was an innovator, a flamboyant redhead before Dennis Rodman, who would have fit in snugly with the NBA's "I Love This Game" mentality, a player everyone loved to watch because of his relentless competitiveness.

"People said he had the heartbeat of a mouse, 200 beats a minute," said Howard Vernon Jr., now principal of City High School in Iowa City, and formerly one of Murray's coaching contemporaries at East Waterloo High School in Iowa. "He just went 100 percent, full bore all the time. The man would never stop."

In a way he has. Now 68, he took an early retirement at age 62 following an outstanding high school coaching and teaching career in Waterloo, and says he loves having the time to himself.

In a way he hasn't. The competitive juices that led him to success as a player and as a coach are still flowing freely. They've just been re-routed to a different sport, tennis, which he plays five times a week. "I just have a competitive nature," he said. "I looked forward to every basketball game. I always thought I could outplay the other guy. I'm that way now. I'm 68 and I think I could beat John McEnroe in tennis."

Though Murray didn't begin playing tennis regularly until he was 35, he won the Iowa Open Championship for players 55 and over in 1988. He was 61. Usually, he competes against even younger players. "Age doesn't mean anything," he said. "I play people 25 to 30 years younger than me."

If he never let size stop him in basketball, why should he let age slow him down in tennis?

He made it to the NBA in 1949-50, playing 56 games and averaging 7.7 points and 1.9 assists for the Tri-Cities Blackhawks. One of his two coaches that season was Red Auerbach.

The Blackhawks went on to Milwaukee as the Hawks in 1951, then to St. Louis in 1955, and finally to Atlanta in 1968-69. Murray, Charlie Criss and Spud Webb all played for the same franchise.

Auerbach went on to fame with the Boston Celtics. He is second in the NBA in career wins behind Atlanta's Lenny Wilkens, but Auerbach was a bust in Tri-Cities. He replaced Roger Potter after a 1-6 start, and went 28-29 the rest of the season, his only losing season in 17 years of coaching in the NBA. "He was a hell of a coach, a bright guy with a brilliant basketball mind," Murray said. "I got along with him okay, but I don't think Red ever liked the Midwest or the people of the Midwest. People out here to him, I think, were hillbillies and farmers. He was from the big city (Brooklyn, New York), and that was his life."

Murray's life was basketball. And playing in the Midwest was always just fine with him.

Murray was born December 12, 1926, the youngest of four children of James and Ruth Wier, in Grand View, Iowa, near the Mississippi River and 40 miles southeast of the University of Iowa. His mom turned 101 last year. "She's in a nursing home," Murray said. "She's still very sharp mentally. She gives me hell for general purposes, for having her in a nursing home. As long as she's doing that, I know she's all right."

Growing up during the Depression was as sobering as one might imagine. "I guess we were all very poor, but I didn't know it," Murray said. "We didn't have anything, but nobody else did either. We sure as hell weren't spoiled because we didn't have anything. People were extremely honest then. Everybody was trying to survive. You could trust people."

Work was wherever any of the Wier family could find it. Murray's dad worked on a farm, then at a pump factory, at an ammunition plant, and then as a maintenance worker for the Iowa Gas and Electric Company. Murray's mom worked in the kitchen of the University of Iowa Children's Hospital, and in a day care facility. Previously, she cleaned at the Grand View School.

They encouraged their children to play sports. Actually, Ruth Wier literally got Murray started in basketball.

After school hours at Grand View, she would sweep up the classrooms. Murray was five and had nowhere to go. "She'd give me a basketball and tell me to go down to the gym," he said. "I could hardly get the ball up to the rim. She'd leave me for an hour."

The time was well spent. Encouraged by his older brothers Ermald and Keith, Murray quickly picked the game up. They hung an old basketball rim on the garage and played endlessly. "It was a neighborhood hangout," Murray said. "We always had kids over there. Drove my dad nuts."

Murray would do the same to opponents. He developed a style of play that worked for him. And he perfected it. "I was an unorthodox player," he said. "I was a slasher. That's just the way I played. I was a one-hand shooter. I was one of the first one-hand shooters. They thought I was crazy, but it's a good shot. You can always get your shot off. Now everybody does it. I shot hook shots. I'd cut across the free throw line and I'd bank 'em in. It looked crazy, seeing someone shooting hook shots from that far out, but it was just natural for me. I was shooting over guys bigger than me. They couldn't block it. You can't block a shot like that."

When Murray was 16, his family moved 10 miles from Grand View to Muscatine, which had a much bigger school. Regardless, Murray excelled in basketball.

He said he really never heard comments that he was too short to play until he went to college. "When I went to Iowa, people said I wasn't big enough to play in the Big Ten," he said. "I didn't pay any attention to them." (Michigan State hadn't yet joined the conference, and it's referred to as both the Big Nine and Big Ten.)

Though he said he was "like most freshmen, scared to death," it didn't take him long to realize he could play major college basketball. Because of World War II, freshmen were allowed to play varsity in Murray's first season at the University of Iowa, 1944-45. Before that season started, Murray more than held his own in pick-up games with varsity players at the Iowa Field House. "I found out then," he said. "I was sure I could play."

Why would a freshman tackle varsity competition right at the start of his first year? "If you start backing off, you're never going to play," he said.

He did, as a freshman, even though the Hawkeyes were loaded and would win the championship of the Big Nine. "I did pretty good," he said. "I was the sixth man. Seven of us would play. I never started, and I shouldn't have. We had five veteran players. I considered myself lucky just to be playing. That was quite a change from high school. The guys were a lot better and bigger."

Regardless, he had his moments. His three late baskets sparked Iowa to a 29-27 win against Michigan. Murray averaged 7.8 points. His scoring average improved to 8.4 as a sophomore, when he had perhaps his greatest moment in college basketball.

Minnesota came to Iowa City unbeaten, January 29, 1946, featuring a line-up which included 6-11 center Jim McIntyre. Players that tall were uncommon in college basketball then.

"They were up the whole game, eight to 10 points," Murray related. "In the last five minutes, the home team rallied. There was under 30 seconds left and we were down four points. I got fouled. I had two free throws and that cut it to two. Then they stalled. With five seconds to go, they got called on a traveling violation. Our guy took it out, threw it to me. I looked for Dick Ives. He was our scorer, but he was running with his back to me and we didn't have much time. I knew I had to get rid of the ball, so I threw it. I took a hook shot from past the free throw circle. I never saw the basket. I was stretched out and trying to get past my guy. I looked up. It hit the back of the rim and went it. The place blew up, went wild. We beat them in overtime."

The score was 63-61. His jubilant teammates carried him off the court on their shoulders. A picture of that made the wire services and was sent around the country. Murray was making a name for himself. The question was, which one?

He was dubbed "The Rampaging Redhead," "Magnificent Murray," and "The Wizard Wier."

A press release from Sports News of the Division of University of Iowa Information Service (Eric C. Wilson was the editor) proclaimed of Murray: "His style of shooting and continual race-horse tactics from the opening whistle until

Murray dribbling for Iowa in 1945.
Courtesy of the University of Iowa

the final gun almost defy description. Undoubtedly he is one of the most unusual players ever to play in the Big Nine.

"His point-making prowess appears to be built around off-balance shots that are amazingly accurate. In fact, many fans have been heard to remark that Wier has to be off-balance to score a field goal. That is an exaggeration. But it typifies the astonishment with which they view their magnificent Murray."

As a junior, Murray's scoring average jumped up to 15.1, a high average considering the much lower-scoring games then. One of his opponents was Minnesota's forward Bud Grant, who went on to coach the Minnesota Vikings in the National Football League.

As a senior, Murray led the nation in scoring at 21.0, with a high of 34 set against visiting Illinois, February 9, 1948, when he made 15 of 33 field goals and four of nine foul shots. His 272 points in 12 Big Nine games was a conference record. He was named MVP of the Big Nine.

"I wouldn't be surprised if Wier is the greatest basketball player in America," his coach, Lawrence "Pops" Harrison, said.

It wasn't a minority opinion. Murray was named First Team All-American, and got to play in the East-West All-Star Game at Madison Square Garden in New York City.

But he and his Iowa teammates were left to forever wonder how their teams would have done in the NCAA or NIT (National Invitational Tournament).

"We were Big Ten champions when I was a freshman," Murray said. "Our only loss the whole year was by one point at Illinois. We qualified for the NCAA Tournament, but we didn't go. Two guys on the team were dental students, and they had a hell of a time getting off from dental college. And one of our best players, Dick Ives, was injured. The coach turned it down. All the guys on that team are still alive. We have a reunion every now and then, and we're still upset."

Then it happened again.

"Our sophomore year, we were leading the Big Ten," Murray said. "Coach got us together and said he turned down an NIT bid because we were leading the Big Ten and we'd get an NCAA bid. Then we got beat in our last two games (at Minnesota and against Indiana). We got nothing. It was very disappointing."

Murray's senior team was 15-4, finishing second in the Big Nine at 8-4 despite losing Dick Ives from the year before. The Hawkeyes could have tied for the Big Nine title, but lost at Michigan in its final conference game.

Regardless, Murray calls college "probably the best time of my life. I was treated outstandingly. I always had good things happen to me."

One was meeting his wife on a blind double date. A close second was being presented a new convertible coupe by fans in Muscatine in April after he finished his senior season.

That officially ended his amateur status. But Murray wasn't done playing basketball. He turned pro. He believes he is the first player from Iowa to play in a major professional basketball league. "Again, it was a hell of an adjustment," he said. "It was a lot rougher."

Murray entered professional basketball at its crossroads.

The forerunner of the NBA, the Basketball Association of America (BAA), was formed in 1946, and had 11 franchises in its first season. The Washington Capitols, Philadelphia Warriors, New York Knickerbockers, Providence Steamrollers, Toronto Huskies and Boston Celtics comprised the Eastern Division. The Chicago Stags, St. Louis Bombers, Cleveland Rebels, Detroit Falcons and Pittsburgh Ironmen played in the Western.

The first game was played November 1, 1946, in Toronto, where the Huskies beat the Knicks 68-66. Any fan taller than 6-8 Huskie center George Nostrand got free admission.

Philadelphia won the initial BAA Championship, four games to one over Chicago.

But the BAA had competition: the National Basketball League, (NBL) which had begun play in 1937 with 13 teams. The NBL shrunk to just four teams in 1943-44, then grew back to 12 in 1946-47. In the summer of 1949, the NBL folded. Six surviving franchises merged into the BAA, which played under a new name that 1949-50 season: the National Basketball Association.

Seventeen teams played in the NBA's first season, 1949-50, but the league cut its number of franchises to 11 the next. Four of the six teams which had been squeezed out of the NBA, the Anderson (Iowa) Packers, Sheboygan (Wisconsin) Redskins, Waterloo Hawks and Denver Refiners, joined four new franchises (the Grand Rapids Hornets, Kansas City Hi-Spots, Louisville Alumnites and St. Paul Lights) to form another league, the National Professional Basketball League (NPBL). By the end of its first and only season, 1950-51, only Sheboygan, Waterloo, Anderson and Evansville (Denver relocated there during the season and changed its nickname to the Agogans) were still playing. Both Sheboygan, which finished first in the Eastern Division at 29-16, and Waterloo, which led the Western at 32-24, claimed the league's championship.

Murray got the distinction of playing in three different leagues in three consecutive seasons on only two different teams. He was with Tri-Cities (the cities of Moline and Rock Island, Illinois, and Davenport, Iowa, on the Mississippi River) for one season in the NBL (1948-49) and the first season of the NBA (1949-50). The following year (1950-51), he played with Waterloo in the NPBL. One of his teammates in Waterloo was Ralph "Buckshot" O'Brien, who also was 5-9. "We were totally opposite," Murray said. "Buck had a quick two-handed shot he could hit from far out. I shot one-handed and drove inside. We complemented each other."

Tri-Cities went 36-28 in the NBL, then 29-35 in the NBA. One of Murray's biggest disappointments in his pro career was during his lone NBA season with Tri-Cities, when the

Blackhawks visited Waterloo. A crowd of more than 8,000 people turned out to see their college hero, Murray, make his NBA debut in Iowa, but Tri-Cities Coach Red Auerbach didn't insert Murray in the game until there were less than two minutes left, despite the fact that Murray had been playing lots of minutes and were the team's fourth leading scorer.

In a 1993 story in the *Des Moines Sunday Register* about Waterloo's one-year tenure in the NBA (1949-50), reporter Jack Hovelson wrote of the game:

"With the Hippodrome packed beyond capacity, the fans waited for Wier's debut. Waited and waited and waited. The game ticked down to its final minutes. Finally, with less than two to play, Wier was sent in...Auerbach never confessed, but it was obvious to 8,000 people in the Hippodrome that he had jabbed his Waterloo tormenters by giving them only a sip of what they came to see."

Actually, a lot of Murray's expectations weren't fulfilled in that single NBA season: "In college, I was used to doing a lot of shooting. With Tri-Cities, I didn't get a lot of shots. But we had real good crowds at Wharton Field House in Moline. On the road, we got $5 meal money, but you could get a great meal for a buck seventy-five. We traveled by train quite a bit. Sometimes we drove in three or four cars. We went all over the damn country. We played a lot of exhibition games. Most of the places we played in were pits. You wouldn't put a dog in them. If they [today's players] had to play just one week the way we did, they'd quit. But it was just getting started. Nobody thought a whole lot about it. You just accepted that was it."

Or you didn't. After his season in Waterloo, the NPBL folded and Murray faced an important moment of his life. He could try to catch on with an NBA team in another city or stay in Waterloo, where he'd been offered a job as a coach and teacher at East Waterloo High School for a little more than half of the $6,000 salary he had made with the Waterloo Hawks. Murray and his wife, Marjorie, who were married in

1948 after meeting in college, had two children then (Terry and Sandra; Marcia, Jeffrey and Sally would follow). "I figured I needed some stability," Murray said. "I had two kids. So I took the job offer. I made the right choice. I was there 38 years."

He taught physical education for one year there, then history, a love since he was a schoolboy, for 37. He served as athletic director for 35 1/2 years. Before he turned to coaching tennis for 10 years, he coached varsity basketball for 24, compiling an outstanding record of 372-140 and winning one state championship.

One of his best players was Mike Woodley, who also starred in football and is now an assistant football coach at Iowa State. "I think the key to Murray Wier is his burning desire to win," Woodley said. "He's probably the most competitive person I've been around in my entire life. When I was a sophomore, he brought me up to varsity at point guard to take his son Terry's place. That tells you how committed he was. He told me afterwards his wife didn't speak to him for a while after that."

Woodley has always talked to him: "He was like a second father to me. He still is."

Maybe that's why Murray let him see something he rarely displayed: how great a ballplayer he was. "He never showed players how he played," Woodley said. Murray made an exception when Woodley was injured. "He made me come in early and after practice, and he'd help me shoot," Woodley said. "He was known for his running jump shots and hook shots. He was ahead of his time in his showmanship."

But the bottom line was always: win. "I love him," Woodley said. "Every winter, he's got five kids and they get together and have a tennis tournament. It's blood and guts. They're all the same way. They're real competitive people. It's the damnedest thing."

Howard Vernon Jr. was hired by Murray as football coach at East Waterloo High School, then became Murray's boss when he was named principal there. "I worked with him for 11 years," Vernon said. "One of the things about Murray was that when he played, he was a tremendous offensive threat. When he became a coach, he was adamant on developing a strong defensive team. The man all was business. You couldn't even see into the gym when he practiced. He put paper over the windows. He wanted them to concentrate 100 percent. And they did. His practices were very intense."

So were his games.

Ritually, he would wear a green corduroy jacket. "It was the ugliest thing I've ever seen," said Gary Hveem, who was Murray's assistant coach for two seasons and is now athletic director at City High School in Iowa City. "He would wear it every game. At some point during a game, that jacket was going to come off. He was either going to stomp on it or throw it into the stands."

Hveem didn't know how Murray would react when one of their players opened the second half of a playoff game by scoring two points off the jump ball at the wrong team's basket. "The place goes crazy," Hveem said. "Murray's coat comes off. Flies into the stands. Called a timeout. The kid didn't know what to say, or what was going to happen. Murray just looks up to the kid and says, 'That was a hell of a shot. Let's try to do it at our end.'"

Most of the time they did.

In his first year as head coach at East Waterloo, 1952-53, he took the Trojans to the state tournament for the first time in 18 years. His 1959-60 team advanced all the way to the state championship game, losing to Marshalltown by 10 points. In 1973-74, East Waterloo won the state title, beating Wahlert of Dubuque, 71-54. "I thought we were good enough to win the championship," he said. "I was surprised we won by that many points."

All told, Murray's teams won or shared in their Big Eight Conference title 14 times in his 24 seasons, including seven in a row, and appeared in the state tournament eight times.

"I had a lot of success," Murray said. "The kids I had worked awfully hard defensively and on rebounding. We were pretty good at it. I had good kids who were willing to do what you wanted."

And, as he had never been preoccupied with his own size, he wasn't with his players' either: "We had all sizes. I never even mentioned size to them. The best players played. I didn't care if they were small. A ballplayer is a ballplayer."

He sure was.

Statistics

Murray Wier

Collegiate

Season	Team	G	Avg Pts	FG Pct	FT Pct
1944-45	Iowa	17	7.8	-	-
'45-46	Iowa	18	8.4	-	-
'46-47	Iowa	18	15.1	.302	.667
'47-48	Iowa	19	21.0	.354	.698

NBA

Season	Team	G	Avg Pts	Avg Ast	FG Pct	FT Pct
1949-50	Tri-Cities	56	7.7	1.9	.327	.693

Buckshot
5-9

R alph "Buckshot" O'Brien had a problem before his first NBA game at famed Madison Square Garden in 1951. He couldn't get in the building. At 5-foot-9, he didn't look the part of an NBA player.

"I'd lost my player's pass," Buck said. "The guard wouldn't let me in. He said he's been on that gate 25 years and he wants to know whose bag I was carrying. At that time, there was a $50 fine for being late on the court."

Fortunately for Buck, his Indianapolis Olympians Coach, Herm Schaefer, happened to be nearby. He was laughing. But he finally told the guard that this 5-9 young man was his guard on his basketball team.

Buck scored 18 against the New York Knicks that night, and paid his respects to the guard afterwards: "I said:
'Did you see the game?'

'Yes sir.'

'If I come in next time, will you let me in with or without a pass?'

'Yes, I will.'"

Such are the tribulations of being one of the 10 shortest players in NBA history.

"They'd call me the runt, the midget, little boy," he said.

They called him something else, too: good. Real good. He was a spectacular scorer at Butler University and averaged a solid 9.0 points, playing in 64 of 66 games for the Olympians in his first NBA season, 1951-52, then 4.9 points in 55 games in the '52-53 season he split with Indianapolis, the Fort Wayne Pistons and the Baltimore Bullets.

Then he walked away from the game at the age of 26 to be with his wife, Doris, and their baby, Mark. He chose family over basketball. He became an insurance man, and excelled at that, too.

Unusual, this man. Special, too. In 1975, he was one of five former athletes chosen for the NCAA Silver Anniversary Award, which recognizes student athletes who have distinguished themselves since completing their college athletic careers 25 years ago. Also honored at a luncheon that year was President Gerald Ford, who'd been named recipient of the Theodore Roosevelt Award, presented to a nationally renowned citizen who played varsity sports in college. Roosevelt played a key role in the creation of the NCAA in 1906.

The other four Silver Anniversary Award winners that year were Robert S. Folsom, the Chairman of the Board of Robert S. Folsom Investments, Inc.; Captain Phillip Joseph Ryan of the U.S. Navy; William J. Keating, a former Congressman and President and CEO of the *Cincinnati Enquirer*; and Billy Mac Jones, president of Memphis State.

At a luncheon attended by 1,400 at the Sheraton-Park Hotel in Washington, D.C., January 7, 1975, Buck was presented his award. "It was a once-in-a-lifetime experience," he told reporter Thomas R. Keating from the *Indianapolis Star*.

"I couldn't believe I was sitting at the head table with the President of the United States.

"I kept thinking about people like Everett Kelly of the Lauder Boys Club who helped me so much when I was young. And Jimmy Doyle, my teammate at Butler who sacrificed himself and gave up the ball and let me be an All-American, and, of course, [Butler Coach] Mr. Tony Hinkle, who did so much for me I can't even mention it all."

Hinkle said: "Buckshot came up the hard way and made something out of himself in many ways. He was a small boy who made it in a big man's game, and he was a poor boy who made himself wealthy. The NCAA honor couldn't have been better placed."

Not bad for a boy destined to be "no bigger than a buckshot," an eighth grader advised to repeat his school year to grow and to work on a stretching machine. He was 4-foot-8 and weighed 84 pounds.

He declined. "I said, 'Hey look, whatever He's given me, He's given me,'" Buck said. "When it was time for me to grow, I did. I went from 4-8 to 5-5 in two years."

He was given his nickname at the age of four by Otto Dickerson, who owned a grocery store on the West Side of Indianapolis.

He was the youngest of 13 children—eight brothers and four sisters—born April 8, 1928, in Henshaw, Kentucky. His dad, Oscar Bennett O'Brien, was 6-foot-1. His mom, Myrtle Winningham, was 5-3. His twin brothers, Walter and Waller, who were Ralph's college teammates at Butler, were 6-1 1/2, and another brother, Pete, was 6-1.

Oscar O'Brien was a farmer in Kentucky. When Buck was two, his dad moved the family to Indianapolis, where he worked his way up to be a foreman at a cotton mill.

"If they had labeled us, they would have said we were in the ghetto in Indianapolis," Buck said. "Back then, everybody was poor."

He was a toddler while the Depression ripped apart America. Yet at the ripe old age of six, he discovered the center of his world for the next 20 years of his life: basketball.

Buck went to the Lauter Boys Club daily after school. It was only three blocks from grade school and only a mile and a half from home. He had few options there: pool, ping-pong or basketball. With the help of Everett Kelly, who ran the club and coached the basketball team there, young Buck began playing hoop. "Soon as school was out, I'd be there from three to five," Buck said. "As I got older, I played more." He'd also go back to the Boys Club three or four nights a week from seven to nine with his older brothers.

Eventually, Buck worked at the club through his college years and became the assistant director there.

He started on his freshman team and then moved up to varsity as a sophomore for the Washington High School Continentals. He was the leading scorer in Indianapolis and named all-city, all-Marion County and All-State as a senior.

He was recruited by Florida, Miami of Ohio, Anderson College, Drake and Butler.

He decided to go to Butler University in Indianapolis—Coach Hinkle used a system there where small guards could play—and by the end of his brilliant career, felt he had made a statement about his height: "They said I was too small in grade school. They said, 'He can't play.' Same scenario in high school. So I played four years, and after I got out, I still heard it all the time. I think it motivated me, because I was just going to prove them wrong. I had too many coaches that said I was too small. Well, I played four years in college and we stuffed those teams' butts. I'd say to their coach:

'Do you remember me?'

'Yes, I'm afraid so. We do make mistakes.'

'Well, everybody makes mistakes.'"

Truth is, Buck didn't make many in college. In the classroom, he graduated in the top 10 in the College of Education. On campus, though he lived at home, he was elected president of his junior class and director of the student council. And on the court, he was a two-time All-American. He also played on Butler's baseball and track and field teams.

He got a break in his freshman basketball season in 1946-47. In the aftermath of World War II, freshmen were allowed to play varsity. Buck started with low expectations, but they quickly dissipated: "I just hoped to make the traveling squad, but it sure got exciting when Mr. Hinkle gave me a starting job."

Then everybody got excited just watching Buckshot play.

He'd lead Butler to a 60-30 record in his four years, setting a school record for points in one season (364) and breaking it himself (420) the next. He led the Bulldogs in scoring in his final three seasons, averaging 11.9, 15.8 and 18.3 points. Those numbers are better than they sound in the '90s because games were much lower scoring when Buck was in college. The two years after Buck graduated, Orvis Burdsall led Butler in scoring by averaging 10.9 and 10.8 points.

Buck was two-time MVP of the Mid-America Conference and a two-time Consensus All-American, honored by *Collier's* and *Look* magazines. He got named to the Little College All-American Team—for players under six feet—for each of his four seasons.

He played in the East-West College All-Star Game, the College-Pro All-Star Game and the College All-Americans-Harlem Globetrotters Game.

Columnist Paul Neville wrote in the *Chicago Tribune* of Buck: "Although he can dribble like a demon, fake, pass and pivot out of any jam, it's when "Buckshot" is popping that he pleases the fans. Let him get set for a second and he'll make the nets dance with joy for Butler. When he's hot, which is often, he can rack up points so fast the scoreboard spins, and, if it's an electric board, the lights flash like a tote board at a race track."

Buck's best shot was the two-hand set shot. "I was very fortunate that I could hit a one-hand jumper as well as shooting set," Buck said. "If I couldn't get by them to drive,

Buckshot as a sophomore at Butler University throwing a behind the back pass.
Courtesy of Ralph O'Brien

I'd set in behind a pick and take the set shot. If they fought through the pick, I'd reverse and go down through the key. If they got the ball back to me, I'd take a jump shot or lay it in."

On his initial trip to New York City and Madison Square Garden, he scored 20 points for Butler in a 63-54 win over LIU (Long Island University) before a crowd of 14,000 in his junior year. "My set shot was working perfectly that night," he said.

Later as a junior, in front of 11,461 home fans at the Butler Field House—since renamed Hinkle in honor of the coach—Buck scored 18 in a 68-54 win over Notre Dame, which ended the Bulldogs' string of seven consecutive losses to the Irish.

But just to make sure Buck didn't think too much of himself, Hinkle invited a well-dressed stranger to sit in on a Butler practice late in Buck's junior season. Before practice, Hinkle told Buck the man was from a national magazine and was going to judge whether or not Buck was worthy of being named an All-American. The man took notes and photos to make it look good.

The catch? For the first 20 minutes of practice, not one Butler player passed Buck the ball. "Buckshot was fit to be tied," Hinkle said.

Then the phony writer got up in apparent disgust and left the building.

Then Hinkle told Buck it was a joke. "It took him a while to recover," Hinkle said.

Some teams felt the same way after playing against Buck.

For some reason, he feasted on Ohio State: Buck against the Buckeyes. In the first of two games in his senior season against the Buckeyes, who were ranked No. 1 in the country, he scored 30, but the host Bulldogs came up short, 67-65.

Then at Columbus, in his final collegiate game, Buck had a career high 39, making 19 of 30 field goal attempts to set an Ohio State Coliseum record. His baskets gave Butler leads at 61-60, 63-61 and 65-64 before he fouled out with 54 seconds to go. The crowd gave him an ovation that lasted nearly two minutes. "I've never seen an opposing crowd do that," he said. Without him, though, the Bulldogs again came out losers, 66-65. "I had to sit there and watch us lose," he said. "I felt terrible."

He felt thrilled many times in the Hoosier Classic, which featured Butler, Indiana, Notre Dame and Purdue. He played in the inaugural Classic at the Butler Field House in 1947-48. Butler beat Purdue 52-50, and Indiana beat Notre Dame, 72-46, in the opening round. With 12,500 fans watching the championship game, Buck scored eight points and the Bulldogs defeated Indiana, 64-51.

Butler also won the second Hoosier Classic, taking Indiana, 64-55, and Purdue, 47-43.

In the third, the Bulldogs beat Purdue, 57-52, but went down in the championship game, 68-57 to Indiana. All Buck did before a crowd of 12,597 at Butler was score a then Butler record of 33. The rest of his team scored 24. That was the measure of his talent.

Buck stepped into professional basketball at a volatile period, as the Basketball Association of America, the National Basketball League, the National Basketball Association and the National Professional Basketball League struggled to survive. Only one did: the NBA.

Buck began his rookie pro season in 1950-51 with the Grand Rapids Hornets in the National Professional Basketball League (NPBL), but was traded after a month to the Waterloo Hawks, where he became a teammate of 5-9 Murray Wier.

Buck continued an outstanding season, averaging 15 points a game, and was named NPBL Rookie of the Year.

With Waterloo, he played in the first pro game ever held in the state of North Dakota. He left a lasting image: 31 points in a 99-97 win against the Sheboygan (Wisconsin) Redskins before about 2,000 fans during the Jack Frost Winter Carnival in Fargo. Sheboygan tried four different players on him, 6-foot-5 Wally Osterkorn, 6-2 Max Morris, John Givens and John Pilch.

He scored 24 against the Anderson Packers, and a pro career high of 39 in a 101-94 win against Sheboygan.

In an interview after the season with Angelo "Jimmie" Angelopolous in the *Indianapolis News,* he said, "I had a wonderful time this year, but you always do when you're hitting. I've been taught a lot—a lot that wasn't just basketball, too. I didn't realize there were so many jealousies in pro ball."

The following fall, he was ready to give up on basketball, teach biology, and serve as an assistant cross country and basketball coach at Broad Ripple High School in Indianapolis. Then the Olympians came courting, and he signed with them.

He left his teaching position on October 24, 1951, to join the Olympians for an exhibition game against Fort Wayne in Greencastle, Indiana, some 40 miles away. "I would never have left Ripple if the Olymps were anywhere but in Indianapolis," he said.

At one point in his NBA rookie season, he had made 26 of his first 28 free throws, a percentage of .929. He would have finished ninth in the NBA in free throw percentage (.819) and second the next season (.848), but he didn't have the minimum number of free throws attempted to be listed in the NBA's league leaders.

One night, he was perfect from the foul line (5 of 5) and the field (5 of 5), scoring 15 points in a scant 17 minutes as Indianapolis beat Fort Wayne, 78-63, at Buck's favorite arena, the Butler Field House.

Typically for a home game, he'd get up at 7:30 or 8 a.m., shower "to get the cobwebs out," then have breakfast with his new bride, Doris Jean, his sweetheart since his sophomore year in high school. They were married June 25, 1950, and are still going strong, still deeply in love after 45 years of marriage. "She's just as pretty now as she was then," Buck said.

For breakfast, Buck would have an egg, a piece of bacon and a piece of fresh fruit. "I wouldn't eat bananas," he said. "They lay in your stomach because of the potassium."

He'd breeze through the *Indianapolis Star* and the *Indianapolis News* and try not to think about the game: "I was always anxious to play, because if you're not nervous, if you're not antsy, you're not going to play well. You have to have that adrenaline flowing, but I'd try to keep it under control."

He'd have a steak, a potato and a salad with no dressing at around 5:30, and leave for the game at 6:30. The Butler Field House, where the Olymps played all their home games, was only 15 minutes away. He and Doris would load the car with people going to the game, but Buck would never drive. "I didn't want any tension," he said.

Snow, however, was always welcome. "I always loved it when it snowed," he said. "Even in high school and college, I always had a good night if it was snowing."

As every player does, he found comfort walking from the locker room onto his home court and seeing familiar fans and baskets that he'd practiced on thousands of times. Then he'd prepare for his match-up that night.

One of his toughest assignments was 5-10 Hall of Famer Slater "Dugie" Martin of the Minneapolis Lakers, a team in the process of winning four championships in five years. The powerhouse Lakers featured three other Hall of Famers: 6-10 George Mikan, the NBA's first dominating big man, 6-5 Jim Pollard and 6-7 Vern Mikkelsen.

"Dugie was tough," Buck said. "There was no question about it. He had his quickness and good speed. Dugie was a good outside shooter, but he didn't shoot a lot. He didn't have to because he had his big men underneath."

Buck also played against the Celtics' Hall of Famer, 6-1 Bob Cousy. "One of the toughest I ever played against," Buck said.

Of course, many guards tried to post Buck low. Buck would generally front the man and count on weak-side help from one of his big men. "The forwards would slide over," he said. "I would front the guy instead of going behind him. I wasn't afraid to yell for help. I'll tell you one thing. Most big teammates look after the little fella. They don't want you to get pounded underneath."

One opponent who gave Buck trouble was 6-3 Dwight "Dike" Eddleman of the Milwaukee Hawks and Fort Wayne Pistons. "He knew how to take a little man in," Buck said. "He'd clamp me, make sure he had body contact with me, make sure I was behind him. His vertical leap was unbelievable."

Buckshot (far left) with the Baltimore Bullets during the 1952-53 season.
Courtesy of Ralph O'Brien

In 1952-53, Buck was waived by the Olymps, signed by Fort Wayne three days later, and traded after six weeks to the Baltimore Bullets.

At Madison Square Garden, he had a fine performance off the bench in a 95-94 overtime loss to the Boston Celtics in an NBA doubleheader before 10,002. He hit four baskets in the fourth quarter, and was credited in the newspaper the next day: "He also kept [Bob] Cousy running and otherwise pretty much occupied."

But the best shooting performance of Buck's life was seen only by his Baltimore teammates and their legendary Hall of

Fame Coach Clair Bee. Jack Kerris, a 6-foot-6, 230-pound forward, was part of the package deal with Buck in the trade from Fort Wayne to Baltimore. Kerris told the story:

"Buckshot was a real small man as far as the pro end of the game went. In fact, he was pretty small even for college, but what a dead shot he was. I'll never forget one day in practice. Bucky started shooting his two hand set shot from about 25 feet out. He started on one side of the court and moved around the circle. I saw him start shooting, so I stopped practicing and started counting his shots. It wasn't long before all players had stopped their workouts and watched the little guy shoot. And when you can get one basketball player to stop and watch another, that's really something. I know it sounds unbelievable, but he hit 52 straight shots before he missed. And believe me, it was done under pressure. After Bucky had hit about 30 in a row, the rest of the boys started to razz him. You know, needle him on every shot. But he just kept firing away. I think he finally missed because he was tired. Clair Bee called it the greatest shooting exhibition he had ever seen."

Buck said, "We were all getting ready to scrimmage, and they said let's have a shoot-around. I started going around the horn, and when I got to 25, all the other players came down to my end of the court and started giving me raspberries. It was fun. When I missed, I said, 'That's it, boys, you'll never see that again.'"

Soon after, Buck left the game he loved, though his pro salary had climbed from $5,250 to $7,200. "I had my son, Mark," Buck said. "I thought this might not be the life to raise a kid, traveling by train all the time. I was 26 years old. I was probably at my prime. It was not an easy decision to make. But I gave it up. With the baby, and the family, I knew I could come back to Indianapolis and get in a business while I was still on top and have the respect of the people."

That has never been a problem for Ralph "Buckshot" O'Brien.

Though he also dabbled as a TV college basketball analyst for WLW 1, Channel 13 in Indianapolis, from 1962 through '68—he would diagram plays on a "Buck Board"—his livelihood was as a general insurance agent for Franklin Life Company. He was typically successful and became a life member of the one million dollar Round Table—the highest honor in the business, signifying at least one million dollars sold per year. He did it for 27 years.

He's semi-retired now—though still selling a bit of insurance—and living with Doris in Clearwater Beach, Florida. Their eldest son, Mark, 41, works in a consulting firm in Indianapolis. Buck's other son Randy, 39, is the Vice President in charge of marketing with Franklin Life in Springfield, Illinois. Mark and Randy's sister, 36-year-old Kyle Jean Stevens, was one of the top women's golfers in the world, having won an NCAA team and individual championship at SMU (Southern Methodist University) and was named 1980 Rookie of the Year in the Ladies Professional Golf Association (LPGA).

Buck's greatest honor was the NCAA Silver Anniversary Award in 1975. In 1987, Buck was inducted into the Indiana High School Hall of Fame. He was elected to the Butler University Hall of Fame in 1993.

These days, Buck plays golf, swims and walks the beach daily. "The good Lord has been good to me," he said.

Buck, who turned 67 on April 28, 1995, has been good to other people. Always. While on the Indianapolis Boys Club's Board of Directors for three years, he helped build two new centers. He coached teams for eight years at the Boys Club, 16 years in the Tabernacle Presbyterian Church Recreational Program and 20 years in the First Baptist Church Recreational Program. He has an annual charity golf tournament for the First Baptist Athletic Program, which raises from $8,000 to $12,000 a year. He was always active in the Fellowship of Christian Athletes and the YMCA. And he's

been county and assistant state chairman of the Heart Fund.
With life, as in basketball, he's always given it his best shot.

Buckshot (back row, middle) with his unbeaten seventh and eighth
grade basketball team at the Lauter Boys Club.
Courtesy of Ralph O'Brien

Statistics

Ralph O'Brien

Collegiate

Season	Team	G	Avg Pts
1946-47	Butler	23	9.3
'47-48	Butler	21	11.9
'48-49	Butler	23	15.8
'49-50	Butler	23	18.3

NBA

Season	Team	G	Avg Pts	Avg Ast	Avg Reb	FG Pct	FT Pct
1951-52	Indianapolis	64	9.0	1.9	1.9	.372	.819
'52-53	Ind/FW/Balt.	55	4.9	1.0	1.3	.336	.848

Calvin

5-9

Calvin Murphy never got it. He never understood that he was too small to play basketball in the NBA: "It didn't dawn on me. I thought the best players played: midgets, giants, whatever. I never looked at myself as a little guy. I played basketball."

On November 15, 1970, just after the start of his NBA rookie season, *Sports Illustrated* put him on the cover, proclaiming to the world: "The Little Man Is Back."

He didn't know the little man had left.

"He didn't care about his size," his Norwalk (Connecticut) High School coach, Jack Cronin, said. "He didn't care if you were 6-5. He'd run right through you."

Utah Jazz President Frank Layden, who coached Calvin for two seasons at Niagara University, in Niagara Falls, New York, concurred: "Calvin didn't think of himself as being small. He thought of himself as being a great, great player."

And he was. But he was never one easily pigeonholed. An athlete who shunned weightlifting, he excelled as a baton twirler. An undersized guard who was a central figure in one of the greatest battles for the national scoring championship in the history of college basketball. A pro basketball player with the same franchise his entire career. An NBA Hall of Famer, an unconscious foul shooter, and an intense, proud warrior at 5-foot-9.

"When I was in high school, everybody was small," Calvin said. "There were a lot of 5-9 players. When I got into college, the talk about my size started. It didn't bother me at all, because I was a cocky little guy. I always had confidence in myself. I never knew anything about size. I got tired of people asking me about it."

He never got tired of playing. "He used to dribble the ball outside on the sidewalk when he came to school," Cronin said. "Rain or cold, he always had a ball in his hands. The high school team only practiced for an hour. He was always the last one out of the gym. He loved to play, and he hated to lose."

Bitterly. Through all the miles his Hall of Fame basketball career has taken him, he still gets worked up about the time he felt he let his Biddy Basketball team down. He was all of 12.

Basketball was in Calvin's genes. His mother, Ina Miller, played for a team called the Bomberettes. "She taught me to play basketball," he said. "My mother was a tremendous athlete. She's from North Carolina. She was one of the great shooters to come out of the South."

Calvin, born May 9, 1948, was the oldest of Ina's seven children. She is 5-foot-11; Calvin's biological father, James, was 5-10. Calvin's two brothers, Bob and Sam Miller, (whose biological father is 6-1 Robert Miller), are each 6-4. "Sammy was the best of the three of us," Calvin said. "He played at Washington State." Bob followed Calvin at Niagara.

Calvin's cousins could play, too. Reginald Steir and his brother David were schoolboy legends in Connecticut before Calvin arrived.

Calvin demonstrated his prowess with a baton long before he could shoot a basketball. "Twirling was a part of my family," he said. "My aunts all twirled. My Aunt Freida started me. My aunt and I were on the Ted Mack show and won. I was five years old."

He competed at the 1964 World's Fair in Queens, New York, when he was 16, and won the military marching event, finished second in the two-baton competition, and third in the solo. He twirled for his high school band for three years and for the Buffalo Bills.

He believes twirling helped his career immensely, as opposed to, say, working out with weights. "I was a very strong athlete," he said. "I never lifted a weight in my life. Twirling gave me hand and eye coordination. It gave me strength. It helped my dexterity. I was a national champion twice. No question it helped my coordination."

And there was no question he was blessed with talent on a basketball court. He displayed it on a national stage at an early age. He was 10 years old when his Biddy Basketball team went to the World Championships, where it lost to Gary, Indiana, in sudden death.

Two years later, his life was imprinted by failure, a failure he still feels: "The biggest disappointment in my basketball career was that we had the best Biddy team in the nation. I had a horrible game when I was 12. That cost us a chance to go to the World Championships. We were the pride and joy of our small city, and I had the worst game of my life. I screwed it all up. I was averaging 30 or 40 points a game. I had 6 in that game. I just had a bad game. I played terrible. I cost my teammates a chance to get to the championships. As a kid, it bothered me all the way through my adolescence."

Or longer.

Greatness can carry a price.

"When he was growing up, he was just driven," Calvin's brother, Bob Miller, head guidance counselor at Briggs High School in Norwalk, said. "He was very committed. He'd play every day. We'd be shoveling the snow off the court so he could shoot jump shots every day. Once he commits himself, he goes 100 percent. He'd be out there shooting at five in the morning. After school, we'd come home. We'd be doing dishes, go out and play some more. It paid off."

Bob calls Calvin and his other brother Sam his best friends. Sam is a phys ed teacher in Norwalk. "We were very fortunate to have a role model like Calvin to follow," Bob said.

Calvin excelled in all sports, especially basketball and football. His boyhood heroes were guards of the NBA: Oscar Robertson, Jerry West, Hal Greer, Archie Clark and Earl "The Pearl" Monroe. "I was like any kid," Calvin said. "Watch a game and just go out and practice."

He wasn't like any kid. He outdid one idol, Clark—a great guard for six different NBA teams—by joining his other idols in the Hall of Fame. "The Lord gave me talent, but I had to work at it," Calvin said. "I was fortunate that I was the proper weight at the right age. My mother and Jack (Cronin) were teachers."

Cronin, retired now and living in Florida, remembers the first time he saw Calvin play. He'd heard about him as a player in junior high. "I saw him for about three minutes," Cronin said. "I said, 'That's enough. That's all I want to know.' He had all the assets. All he had to do was corral them."

Sometimes it wasn't easy teaching this spectacular schoolboy athlete. "He was making 55 or 60 points a game," Cronin said. "The other team used to play keep-away. We had to foul them to get the ball. He wanted to shoot. I set him down a couple of times because he got a little angry."

Calvin remembers one time vividly: "He sent me to the showers in one game in the second quarter because I was

High-jumping Calvin of Niagara University against Thomas More.
Courtesy of Niagara University

being a jerk. I was a sophomore, and we were playing New Canaan. He sent me home. He tells the story now why he did it. He knew with me, the sky was the limit."

That night, the coach and his player both wondered how the star scorer would react. "He didn't sleep that night," Calvin said. "I didn't either. He didn't know if I'd be at practice the next day. I was out there the next day an hour early. I was in his office. I wanted to get back into his good graces. Big time. He's been raising me ever since."

Along the way, Cronin watched one of the greatest foul shooters in the history of the NBA develop. "The only guy who beat him was me," Cronin said. "We shot after the practices for quarters. We'd shoot without looking at the basket. It was no fun looking. Afterwards on the bus, he'd say, 'You owe me some quarters.' I'd say, 'No, you owe me some.'"

Calvin professes no foul shooting secrets: "It was just like anything else. I learned the basics and I practiced it. It was nothing I singled out."

He'd be singled out in college. In every single game he played.

Calvin, then 5-6 1/2, put up extraordinary numbers and led Norwalk to a 27-1 record and state championship his senior year, 1965-66. Among the some 200 colleges which recruited him were Providence, Villanova, Boston College, Holy Cross, Maryland and Niagara. Ed Donohue, who would move on to become head coach and athletic director at King's College (in Wilkes Barre, Pennsylvania) in 1968, recruited Calvin for Niagara, and he chose to play there.

Back then, freshmen weren't allowed to play varsity basketball. So Calvin spent his first season at Niagara averaging 48.9 points for the freshman team in 19 games.

As amazing as he was, word came out of two other spectacular freshmen that 1966-67 season. Their last names, as did Calvin's, started with 'M': Pete Maravich at LSU and Rick

Mount of Purdue. Maravich was 6-5 and Mount 6-4, but, just as Calvin, were outstanding outside shooters. "Pistol Pete" Maravich averaged 43.6 points for LSU's freshman team, and Mount 35.0 for Purdue's.

Their names would be linked forever: consensus First Team College All-Americans in 1968-69 and '69-70. In '66-67, Maravich had been named to the First Team, Calvin to the Second and Mount not at all.

They would come to define college basketball by the time they were done, and still stand today as the first (Maravich), fourth (Murphy) and seventh (Mount) NCAA All-Time leaders in career scoring average at 44.2, 33.1 and 32.3, respectively. Maravich, who died suddenly at the age of 40 in 1988, would star in the NBA, too, and reach the Hall of Fame. Mount had a less visible pro career in five seasons with four different teams in the ABA.

In college, the huge number of points the trio kept producing was astounding. "I didn't realize how much of a side show we had become," Calvin said. "Pistol became the greatest scorer in the history of the game. I could have, but Frank Layden changed that. He had a team concept. I got to know Pistol. To be talked about with him was an honor.

"I got to know him at the '68 Olympic Trials [where Calvin was cut] in Albuquerque. We became friends instantly. Mutual respect. He was a down-to-earth guy, a people guy. Over the years, playing against him, we got even closer. I didn't have to be a bad actor to play hard. I've always respected talent. The old school didn't want you to be friends with the opponent. I never want to be enemies with anybody."

But he was. Ask anyone who tried covering him on defense in college.

"I was blessed with a lot of quickness," Calvin said. "I had the total package offensively. I could shoot the ball off the dribble. I could shoot the ball off picks. I was much quicker than the other guards. I had a variety of shots. I shot a running hook shot. I penetrated. I absolutely had no problem ever scoring. Never. In college, I ran into every defense known to man: the man to man, the zones, the diamond and one, box and one, everything you can think of. I had teammates that spent all day getting me open. If I had to do that on my own, it would have tired me out."

Instead, he tired whole teams out.

With *Sports Illustrated* on hand to cover his first collegiate game, he began the 1967-68 season by scoring 41 against LIU (Long Island University), but the Purple Eagles lost, 84-79.

So Calvin scored 57 the next game against Villa Madonna (the Kentucky school was renamed Thomas More), shattering Al Butler's school record of 49 set seven years earlier. Butler, then coach of Niagara's freshman team, was on hand to watch Calvin demolish his record.

Calvin followed with 41 against Bowling Green, 52 vs. LaSalle, 42 against Cornell and 41 vs. Valparaiso. But Niagara wasn't winning.

In a showdown in nearby Olean, New York, against a 10-0 St. Bonaventure team led by future Hall of Fame center Bob Lanier, Calvin scored "only" 25 and Niagara was crushed, 101-72.

At the mid-point of the season, Niagara was 5-6, and Head Coach Jim Maloney announced that he would resign at the end of the year.

Two nights later, Calvin scored 48 against Canisius. He had 42 vs. Providence, 36 against DePaul and 42 against St. John's in a bitter 74-73 loss.

Then Calvin soared even higher, posting 50 points three times in 12 nights in February vs. St. Peter's (New Jersey), Buffalo and Syracuse.

That was 150 points in three games by a guard in two weeks. Incredible. His 50 against Syracuse led to a 116-107 win.

Calvin scored 41 in a return match with Canisius. Yet the Purple Eagles finished 12-12.

Calvin averaged an astounding 38.2 points and wasn't even that close to Maravich, who checked in at 43.8 to lead the country. Maravich averaged 44.2 and 44.5 his following two seasons. They still rank 1-2-3 in all-time.

As Calvin's sophomore season wound down, rumors were heard that he was thinking of changing schools. Fortunately for Frank Layden, who took over as Niagara Coach in 1968-69, Calvin remained, leaving Layden joyous: "I inherited him. Calvin was a machine, a physical machine. He never got tired. And that was one of his greatest assets. He wore people down."

Layden coached his first college game, December 7, 1968, at Niagara's Gallagher Center, named after long-time Niagara Coach John "Taps" Gallagher. Calvin took 46 shots from the field against Syracuse and made 24 of them. He was 20 of 23 at the foul line, scoring 68 points in a 118-110 win, at the time the No. 1, and now still the third highest scoring total against a Division I opponent in college basketball history. Only Kevin Bradshaw of U.S. International (72), and Maravich (69) have ever scored more.

The evening was especially sweet for Calvin. His mom was at the game. And, the year before at Niagara, Syracuse played a slowdown game—remember, no shot clock back then—limiting Calvin to 15 points and stealing a 50-49 overtime decision.

"The 68 was against Syracuse," Layden pointed out. "It wasn't chopped liver. I told my wife driving home, 'I think I'm going to like college coaching.'

"He was so good, I couldn't screw him up."

Four nights later, Calvin netted 44 against Cornell. Later in his junior year, Calvin lit up Indiana for 47 points, Columbia for 47, Iona for 42 and Fairfield (Connecticut) for 39. He averaged 32.4 points, but Niagara finished 11-13.

His senior year would be different. Calvin topped 40 just once—49 against Thomas More. He averaged 29.4 points a game, and Niagara had an outstanding season. The Eagles opened 7-0, then won the Oklahoma City University Tournament, the nation's oldest Christmas holiday tournament, by beating Rice, Tennessee and Oklahoma City, upping their record to 10-0.

In a late-season win against St. John's, Calvin was fouled with 14 seconds left and Niagara down one point. "He just stepped up and made the two foul shots," Layden said.

In his final home game, though, Calvin scored just 14 against Canisius. Niagara won anyway, 60-57.

In its first and only appearance in the NCAA Tournament thanks to an at-large bid because of its 21-5 record, Niagara was matched with Ivy League winner Penn, which was 25-1, in the Eastern Regional. Layden learned that the Quakers were so confident that they would win that they made room reservations and menu selections in Columbia, South Carolina, for the next round of the Tournament. "Let's go out and beat them and sleep in their rooms and eat their food," Layden told his club. Niagara did, upending the Quakers 79-69.

That's as far as the Eagles got, though. Villanova took them out 98-73, and, in a consolation game, North Carolina State beat them 108-88. Calvin scored 35 in his final college game, concluding his career with 2,548 points, fifth all-time. At the start of the 1994-95 college season, he'd slipped to 34th, but the inception of the three-point field goal in 1987 has forever changed the meaning of scoring records. Regardless, Maravich is still No. 1 (3,667). One can only imagine the numbers he, Calvin and Rick Mount would have posted if their deadly deep, outside shots were worth 3 points rather than 2.

In his glorious college career, Calvin had scored 30 or more in 42 of 77 games, 40 or more 13 times and 50 or more six times. His uniform number (23) was retired.

The '69-70 season ended a storied period for college basketball in the Buffalo area. Niagara was 22-7, St. Bonaventure 25-4, and upstart Buffalo State, featuring future NBA star Randy Smith, was 21-5.

One of Calvin's admirers in college was Rudy Tomjanovich, now the head coach of the Houston Rockets. Tomjanovich, who would wind up a roommate and teammate of Calvin for 11 seasons, and godfather to one of his children, was an

All-American himself at the University of Michigan. In those pre-ESPN TV nights, one couldn't watch practically every great player in the country on a nightly basis. Tomjanovich had read about Calvin and wanted to find out if he was for real: "My buddies and I jumped in a car, and went to the University of Detroit one night just to check him out. We weren't disappointed, either."

Calvin was, though, the day of the 1970 NBA Draft.

Despite all that he had accomplished, he was not taken until the second round, when the San Diego Rockets, who would relocate in Houston the following season, made him the 18th player picked—there were only 17 NBA teams then. Guess who the Rockets took with the No. 2 selection in the first round. Rudy Tomjanovich.

"My feelings were hurt," Calvin said. "I was First Team All-American. I wasn't picked until the second round because of the size thing."

The shock of not being picked in the first round alarmed him: "I wouldn't have the luxury of being able to wait my turn to fit in. I had to come into the NBA and make an impact quickly. Alex Hannum let me do it."

Hannum, who had coached 5-9 Larry Brown at Oakland in the ABA in 1968-69, had been named coach of the Rockets early in the 1969-70 season, inheriting a 9-17 club from Jack McMahon. The Rockets finished 27-55, and Hannum wanted changes for the '70-71 season. One, despite prevalent wisdom, would be 5-9 Calvin Murphy.

"I consider Alex Hannum the guru of bringing the small guy back into the game," Calvin said. "He said, 'Screw the size. He can play.'"

Hannum was right.

"One of his [Calvin's] handicaps is it takes him so long to come down," Hannum deadpanned to *Sports Illustrated* in 1970. "There was a time when they thought the age of even the 6-2 guard was over...But there are a lot of 5-9 athletes around, so why is Calvin going to make it? He's got intelligence

and character. He has strength, both physically and socially—
he's a good citizen on the team. People like him. He's a good
person. He loves his family and wants to do something in
life."

Calvin with the Houson Rockets.
Courtesy of the Houston Rockets

Calvin played in all 82 games in his first NBA season, without starting in a single one, and averaged 24.6 minutes, 15.8 points and 4.0 assists. He was named to the All-Rookie Team and finished fourth in Rookie of the Year balloting— Geoff Petrie of Portland and Dave Cowens of the Celtics dead heated for the award. Tomjanovich averaged 5.3 points and 5.0 rebounds. He and Calvin would lead the Rockets, who improved to 40-42 in their final season in San Diego, for the ensuing decade.

Calvin found ways to compensate for his lack of size on defense: "I was a pest. I was fairly strong so I couldn't be bullied. I would pick up my player full court. If they tried to post me, I fronted them. I loved when they took me down low because I would bang the hell out of them. Then they stopped taking me low. If you took me low, you had to pay the piper. There was never a disadvantage for me. That was in the mind of everyone else. Players I guarded complained all the time about me fouling or holding."

A lot of times they were right. In 13 years, Calvin fouled out of 53 of the 1,002 games he played. Only Hakeem Olajuwon has fouled out of more games for the Rockets (74). Through 1995, though Hakeem was closing ground (3,204), Calvin was still No. 1 in Rocket history with 3,250 fouls, an average of more than three per game (3.24). By comparison, Hall of Fame center Kareem Abdul-Jabbar is No. 1 in the NBA in all-time personal fouls with 4,657, but his average is 2.99, and he fouled out of only 48 games, five less than Calvin.

Calvin did what he felt he had to do. "I did the job," he said. "You don't stop anyone in the pros. You contain. There are always mismatches."

While Calvin's style of play refuted the notion that short players couldn't be physical, he also blew away the mental stereotype of the short player as an underdog. "I was always the underdog in the minds of other people, not in mine," he said. "All that is in the figment of the imagination, that because of my size I was an underdog. If you allow yourself to think that way, you're going to lose because that's negative thinking. If you go to the foul line and say you won't make it, you won't. My being successful isn't about me being small. I succeeded because I was talented. I get a lot of mail from the average sized player asking me how they can make it. I tell them, if you think about it that way, you'll never succeed. I heard people say to me, 'Murph, what if you were 6-4? You would have been bitchin'.' I say, 'At 6-4, I couldn't do anything more. I made the Hall of Fame.'"

He earned his way.

Though he started only 585 of his 1,002 games, he remains—at least for a while until Olajuwon passes him—the Rockets' all-time leading scorer (17,949 points) and sixth in career scoring average (17.9). He is second in all-time Rockets' free throw percentage (.892 over 13 seasons compared to Rick Barry's .941 for two), first in assists, second in steals and first in games and minutes played.

His most productive season was in 1977-78, when he finished fifth in the league in scoring (25.6) behind 6-7 George Gervin (27.2), 6-4 1/2 David Thompson (27.1), 6-9 Bob McAdoo (26.5) and 7-2 Kareem Abdul-Jabbar (25.8).

Calvin went on a tear that season, scoring 41 against Atlanta, January 7, 1978; 46 against Washington, March 10; and then a franchise record 57 against the Nets eight nights later, making 24 of 40 from the field and nine of 12 at the line. He scored 42 against the Jazz, April 7.

In other seasons, Calvin scored 45 against Buffalo, 42 against Denver and 40 vs. Detroit.

Tomjanovich remembers another night, when Calvin scored 42 in Game 7 of the 1981 Western Conference Semifinals against San Antonio. "That night, he was in a coma," Tomjanovich said. "It was a zone I'd never seen before."

Houston won the game, 105-100, then beat Kansas City four games to one to reach the NBA Finals. The Rockets lost to the Celtics in six games.

Calvin against the Knicks.
Courtesy of the Houston Rockets

In 1979-80, Calvin was named for the only time to the NBA All-Star Game, checking in with six points, five assists, four turnovers and two steals.

Surprisingly, he didn't prosper when the NBA adopted the three-point field goal in 1979-80, making only one of 25 tries that season and nine of 47 the next three years.

But Calvin Murphy will never be remembered for missing shots, but making them, especially at the foul line, where he made a higher percentage of free throws than just about everybody who has ever played in the NBA.

He was a good foul shooter in college, .881 as a senior and .849 in his Niagara career.

He was even better in the NBA. "I used free throws as my legacy," he said. "I wanted to do that better than anybody."

Calvin still holds the NBA record for best free throw percentage in one season, when he shot .958, making 206 of 215 shots in 1980-81 (Mahmoud Abdul-Rauf of Denver nearly eclipsed him in 1993-94, shooting .956). Calvin led the NBA that season and in 1982-83, and finished among the top five nine other times. Calvin shot .900 or better five seasons, second only to Rick Barry's seven.

Calvin held the record for consecutive free throws made (78 from December 27, 1979, through February 20, 1980) until Michael Williams made 84 straight with Minnesota in 1993.

And Calvin's career free throw percentage (.892) is still third in the NBA behind Cleveland's Mark Price (.906) and Barry (.900).

He and Tomjanovich are the only Rockets to have their uniform numbers—Calvin's was 23, Rudy's 45—retired.

For the past four years, Calvin has worked as a Rockets' TV analyst for KTXH-TV 20 and for Home Sports Entertainment. Calvin also does clinics and community relations work for the Rockets in their Stay In School Program. "I talk to kids," he said. "I tell them education is the way to go."

It took Calvin four cracks to get into the Hall of Fame, but when he did, May 10, 1993, he was in fine company: Julius "Dr. J." Erving, Bill Walton, Dan Issel, Walt Bellamy, Dick McGuire, Ann Meyers and Ulyana Semyonova of the Soviet Olympic Team.

Walton said, "Calvin Murphy was the best backcourt player I played against. He taught me the nuances of playing basketball."

In his acceptance speech, Calvin said, "What I decided to do was take one word and describe what Calvin Murphy is all about. That word is sacrifice. I'm not talking about the sacrifice I made for myself. I'm talking about what everybody around me did for me."

He listed his mother, family, coaches and teammates.

Reflecting about his life, Calvin said last year: "I never drank. I never smoked. I never stayed out late. I knew just by the way my body felt if I was going to have a good night. I was fortunate in my career, playing with guys that when they saw I was in my rhythm, when I was in my zone, they got me the ball. I've never considered myself a star. I never tried to be a star. I just wanted to be the best I could be."

He was. Maybe, someday, he'll even forgive himself for that one Biddy Basketball Tournament game. Even Hall of Famers can have an off night.

Statistics

Calvin Murphy

Collegiate

Season	Team	G	Avg Pts	Avg Ast	Avg Reb	FG Pct	FT Pct	3 Pt Pct
1967-68	Niagara	24	38.2	-	5.4	.506	.841	-
'68-69	Niagara	24	32.4	-	4.9	.437	.840	-
'69-70	Niagara	29	29.4	-	3.6	.457	.881	-

NBA

Season	Team	G	Avg Pts	Avg Ast	Avg Reb	Abg Stl	FG Pct	FT Pct	3 Pt Pct
1970-71	San Diego	82	15.8	4.0	3.0	-	.458	.820	-
'71-72	Houston	82	18.2	4.8	3.2	-	.455	.890	-
'72-73	Houston	77	13.0	3.4	1.9	-	.465	.888	-
'73-74	Houston	81	20.4	7.4	2.3	1.9	.522	.868	-
'74-75	Houston	78	18.7	4.9	2.2	1.6	.484	.883	-
'75-76	Houston	82	21.0	7.3	2.6	1.8	.493	.907	-
'76-77	Houston	82	17.9	4.7	2.1	1.8	.490	.886	-
'77-78	Houston	76	25.6	3.4	2.2	1.5	.491	.918	-
'78-79	Houston	82	20.2	4.3	2.1	1.4	.496	.928	-
'79-80	Houston	76	20.0	3.9	2.0	1.9	.493	.897	.040
'80-81	Houston	76	16.7	2.9	1.2	1.5	.492	.958	.235
'81-82	Houston	64	10.2	2.6	1.0	0.7	.427	.909	.063
'82-83	Houston	64	12.8	2.5	1.2	0.9	.447	.920	.286

Hershey
5-9 1/2

Step up! Three shots for a quarter! Make one basket and win a prize. Look how easy it is!"

And it was easy for both of the two boys, Sam Carl and his younger brother Howie—better known as Hershey—to demonstrate their facility in making shots from 17 feet away while they were running the basketball concession and hawking the crowd at defunct Riverview Park, the world's largest amusement park, in Chicago in the late 1950s.

The prize for making one of three was a Hawaiian lei. "Get your girlfriend a lei," Hershey or Sam would beckon. Making two got a plastic whistle. All three were worth a plaster kewpie doll. To get a teddy bear, the customer had to make six.

But the biggest winner would be Hershey himself.

Both Carl brothers were outstanding players. Sam, who was seven years older, starred in high school and got a scholarship to the University of Iowa, only to break his ankle in his freshman season, leave school and never return.

Hershey was even better. Following a brilliant schoolboy career, he was good enough to rewrite the scoring records at DePaul after three other major college teams took a look at his height, 5-feet-9 1/2, and said "No way." He found a way. He starred in college and played in the NBA for one bitter-sweet season in his hometown of Chicago.

Thirty-three years later, he remains one of just 10 people under 5-feet-10 to ever play in the NBA.

"He was a little guy who was an extremely fine shooter," his former DePaul coach, the legendary Ray Meyer, said. "The height was always a question, but you always make room for a guy who can shoot the ball."

Not always. Not everywhere.

Carl's father, Morris Kuroyl, emigrated from Russia to the United States just before the first World War at the age of 12. As with thousands of other immigrants, his name was changed at Ellis Island, shortened and Americanized to Carl.

Morris was the vanguard of his family of 10. Once settled in Chicago on Maxwell Street, a haven for Jewish immigrants, he opened a street-side business, selling underwear and gloves. When his business grew, he was able to open an entire clothing store and eventually earn enough money over the next several years to send for his parents and seven siblings.

Carl's mother, Anna Friedman, also came to the United States from Russia, but didn't meet Morris Carl until she became friends with his sister, Pauline. Pauline fixed the two up. They married, had four children, and made a life in America until they both died from cancer six months apart in 1985.

Howie was four years younger than his sister Charlotte and five years older than his second sister, Sandy.

Howie was nicknamed Hershey at the age of five by his friends because his relatives called him Herschel, his Hebrew name, and not because of his sweet tooth and his affinity for Hershey bars.

When Sam demonstrated his considerable ability in basketball, it was quite natural that his younger brother would follow him, and he did, literally, at the midway at Riverview Amusement Park and in pick-up games on the outdoor courts at Eugene Field near their home.

Sam worked at the park during summers operating rides. On his lunch break, he'd always go to the basketball stand, where he got to know the owner. The owner hired Sam when he was 20. Two years later, Sam got Hershey, then 15, a job there, too. Hershey worked there for eight summers, giving him an unlimited opportunity to shoot baskets during slow times, breaks, after hours, any time he could.

One of Hershey's customers was Hugh Heffner. "He used to come by through the park with a girl, blond and beautiful," Hershey said. Heff took one shot and missed.

Hershey practiced free throws from 15 feet away and shots as far as 25 feet. "You couldn't go out too far because you'd be in the midway, but it helped my shot," Hershey said. "It sharpened my eye."

He tried every shot he could devise. He guesses he took more than 20,000 shots in each of his eight summers at the park. And as he, the city of Chicago, and eventually the entire country would find out, Hershey had a lot of natural talent to build on.

His determination was quite evident at a young age. At Eugene Field, where he began playing when he was eight, Hershey didn't let his size stop him, nor did he allow the fact that he was frequently chosen last prevent him from playing against bigger and older kids. He developed head fakes and quick moves to get his shot off against taller players. He dribbled behind his back long before it became popular. He threw no-look passes. And he was relentless. He never stopped coming at you. "He was a very good dribbler, a very good passer and a very good shooter," Sam said. "He could get his shot off any time he wanted to. He was tricky."

Norm Sonju, now the General Manager of the Dallas Mavericks, can testify. The 6-3 Sonju, who played high school ball for North Schurz High in Chicago, had the misfortune of trying to guard Hershey on one of his best nights after Hershey had worn out North Schurz's top scorer, Roger Jenne. By the time he was done with Jenne and Sonju, Hershey had 44 points in a 78-67 win for Von Steuben. "On most of his baskets, it seemed like if someone passed to him past half-court, he'd let it go," Sonju said. "He was just hitting everything. His release was so quick and so low. He would let the thing fly. He was a tremendous outside shooter with great range. He didn't have tremendous quickness, and he wasn't fast, but he just could flat out shoot the ball."

Ira Berkow, author and sports columnist for *The New York Times,* was a year behind Hershey in school in Chicago— Hershey at Von Steuben and Berkow at Sullivan. They played against each other in high school, and as both opponents and teammates in pick-up games at Eugene Field. They became and remain close friends.

"There used to be great games at Field Playground," Berkow said. "The first time I played against him at Field, his legend preceded him. As a sophomore in high school, he was already a legendary player."

Berkow vividly remembers the first time they played together in a pick-up game at Eugene Field: "The first time I ever got a pass from him, I was cutting to the basket on the baseline, and he threw the ball so softly that all I had to was catch it and flip it in. It was such a beautiful, manageable pass. I never had a pass like that. It kind of knocked me out."

Hershey's burgeoning skills knocked out a lot of people, especially the ones who played against him. As a senior at Von Steuben in 1955-56, Hershey averaged 34 points a game to lead the city of Chicago in scoring, but the college scholarship offers never even reached a trickle.

Kansas with Wilt Chamberlain on its team, Bradley University and the University of Illinois expressed some interest. DePaul sent a letter of inquiry, but Carl wanted to play outside Chicago. "At the time, I wanted to experience what being away at college was like," he said.

The experience stunk.

Hershey visited Kansas and Bradley, and, evidently, failed to impress either coaching staff, which hadn't seen him play in high school. "The coaches didn't say I was too short, but I saw the way they looked at me up and down," Hershey said. "I could see that they were surprised, because I was the leading scorer in the city. They never said anything. I left and they never contacted me."

Neither Kansas nor Bradley offered him a scholarship.

What could he do? "You can't add inches," he said. "If they'd seen me play, then maybe it would have been different. Maybe."

Hershey accepted a partial scholarship to Illinois, and that didn't work out well either.

At the time, freshmen weren't allowed to play varsity ball. The last player on the bench for the University of Illinois freshman basketball team in 1956-57 was Hershey Carl. In fact, he was told not to bother to dress for the annual freshman/varsity scrimmage.

He was 18 years old and confronted with a crisis almost every basketball player experiences at some point in his career. When players have similar talent, which players have enough physically and mentally to succeed at a higher level? What separates players on a college team full of former high school all-stars, or a pro team full of ex-college stars? Who can hike his play up to a new standard?

And when does a player concede that he's not good enough or big enough to move on? Does he face the unpleasant reality of his present situation and accept it or defy it?

Hershey could have easily packed it in and come to the same conclusion others had reached for him: he wasn't tall enough to play major college basketball. "I never thought that I wasn't good enough," he said. "It was just a case of not getting an opportunity. It was very frustrating."

He made up his mind before the end of his first semester at Illinois to transfer. What better place to go than back to Chicago at DePaul? "He came to DePaul and we were glad to take him," Ray Meyer said.

Hershey would make Meyer even happier once he put on a DePaul uniform. Hershey could play major college ball. He could be a star.

"He was a little guy who was an extremely fine shooter," said Meyer, whose outstanding 42-year record at DePaul was 724-354. "If he had played with the three-point shot, he'd probably have led the country in scoring." Hershey estimates that three quarters of his shots were behind what's now the three-point line in college basketball.

As it was, he still set records at DePaul. In getting one of them, he outshone George Mikan, the 6-10 Hall of Famer who dominated the early years of the NBA. Mikan still holds the DePaul record for points in a game with 53—set at New York City's Madison Square Garden against Rhode Island in the 1945 NIT—but Mikan's record of 37 points at DePaul's Alumni Hall was erased by a player more than a foot shorter: Hershey.

DePaul moved into the new Rosemont Horizon in 1980, but the Blue Demons occasionally still play a game at Alumni Hall. So Hershey's still standing record of 43 points there—set against Marquette in an 81-78 overtime win, December 23, 1960—could be eclipsed. But it's not likely. Forty-three points remain a huge number for any player in a single game.

Firing all those foul shots at Riverview Park paid off handsomely for Hershey in college. He finished second in the nation in free throw percentage (.875) in 1960-61 —just .002 behind Stu Sherard of Army (.877)—and is still DePaul's all-time career leader in free throw percentage at .853.

But Hershey was much more than an excellent foul shooter. He could score from just about anywhere. Meyer repeatedly ran a play for him, bringing the center outside to set a pick. "And then he'd let it go," Meyer said. "He was so quick getting the shot off. He also had a great move to the basket."

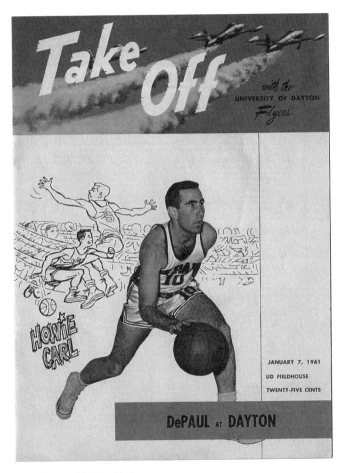

Hershey as DePaul's hero.
Courtesy of DePaul University

Hershey was a hit at DePaul from Day One. In his fourth game, against Bowling Green, December 13, 1958, he made all 10 of his foul shots in a 73-70 win. Then he scored 37 in an 87-70 win vs. Western Kentucky.

Then there was a night during his sophomore season in Buffalo, when DePaul was playing Canisius. Coach Meyer relates: "I took him out because he was shooting too much. I wanted to let him know that we had four other guys. But I had to put him back in the game, and we won (73-67). I taught him a lesson, and he taught me a lesson."

In his junior season, Hershey led a 22-point win against Purdue with 26 points and 12 rebounds. Purdue Coach Ray Eddy said afterwards, "How can you figure this game? The smallest man on the court gets as many rebounds as any." In his game story the next day in the *Chicago Herald American*—since folded—Jim Enright wrote: "The cunning pint-sized Carl did everything but carry the flag and lead the singing of the National Anthem as DePaul crushed visiting Purdue, 87-65, for its fifth straight win of the year last night.

"Racing under and around his bigger teammates and opponents, Carl, a junior at DePaul, compiled nine field goals in 21 shots; eight of 10 free throws, and one-fourth of DePaul's 48 rebounds, 12. What these statistics failed to tell were the countless Purdue passes Carl batted out of reach when unable to complete an interception, or the spark and spice he applied to the pepped-up Demons. His was truly a great one-man gang performance."

He had a sweet moment, even in defeat, at the end of his junior season when DePaul lost to No. 1 ranked Kansas State, 102-70, and 71-65 to Texas Christian University, in the NCAA Midwest Regional Tournament. The games were at the Allen Field House at the University of Kansas. He did play at Kansas after all.

After the season, Meyer informed Hershey that he had been under consideration for the 1960 U.S. Olympic Team. But he didn't get picked, and the team, featuring Oscar

Robertson, Jerry Lucas and Jerry West, won the Olympic Gold Medal in Rome.

But Hershey continued his outstanding collegiate career. Four games into his senior season, he made two jumpers in the final 40 seconds to lead DePaul to a 62-60 win against Bowling Green. He scored 22 that night.

In the next game, he scored his career high 43 against Marquette, making 23 foul shots—still a DePaul record—of 26 attempts. Marquette Coach Eddie Hickey was moved to call Carl the best small player he ever saw. Dayton Coach Tom Blackburn made the same observation.

Against Ohio University, Hershey scored nine consecutive points in a second half spurt to rally the Blue Demons to its 10th straight win, 69-60. He finished with 26 points.

He led the Blue Demons in scoring (19.2, 19.7 and 16.3) and in free throw percentage (.826, .854 and .875), and was named to the Little All-American Team—for players under six feet—in each of his three seasons at DePaul.

At the end of his senior season (1960-61), Hershey was chosen to a College All-American Team of all seniors to tour the country and play 20 games against the Harlem Globetrotters. This wasn't the typical Washington Generals' script of laying down and dying for the Trotters. The collegians beat the Trotters in Cincinnati, April 7, 1961, 89-82, behind leading scorer and Game MVP Hershey Carl. Hershey was also the leading scorer and the MVP of the tour. "We were giving them fits," Hershey said.

The Trotters' owner, Abe Saperstein, was on the verge of beginning a new league to challenge the NBA, the American Basketball League. "He called me up to his hotel room," Hershey said. "He said, 'Kid, I want you to play for my team in Chicago.'"

Hershey was flattered, and flattered again when the ABL's Chicago team, the Majors, drafted him. He'd also been drafted by the Chicago Packers, an expansion team in the NBA. He chose the NBA, a decision he's questioned many times because playing in the NBA in his hometown turned out to be bitterly disappointing. "The American Basketball League had the three-point shot, and I would've gotten more opportunities to play, and maybe to start," Hershey said. But not for long. The ABL folded after a season and a half.

In 1961, the NBA, now at 29 teams, decided to expand from eight clubs to nine. Boston, New York, Syracuse and Philadelphia played in the Eastern Division in '61-62, while the Chicago Packers joined L.A., Cincinnati, Detroit and St. Louis in the Western.

The Packers were given one player from each team in an expansion draft—the caveat being that each team could protect its best players—and the No. 1 pick in the 1961 NBA college draft. The Packers chose wisely by taking center Walt "Bells" Bellamy, who would became an NBA Hall of Famer.

But he wasn't strong enough to carry a completely over-matched team. The Packers would finish 18 and 62, though Bellamy finished second in the NBA in scoring (31.6) to Wilt Chamberlain (50.4) and ahead of such luminaries as Oscar Robertson, Bob Pettit, Jerry West and Elgin Baylor. Bellamy led the league in field goal percentage (.519) and was third (19.0) in rebounding behind Chamberlain (25.7) and Bill Russell (23.6).

Hershey had a different type of season, a season he'd never experienced before, one which finished his basketball career. He hardly played. "It was a horrible experience," Hershey said. "The team was terrible, and I'd never sat on the bench for any length of time. It was a pretty traumatic experience."

Sometimes at the Packers' home games in the Chicago International Amphitheater—"Right next to the stockyards; it literally stunk," Hershey said—the fans would chant, "We want Hershey. We want Hershey." That only made Hershey feel worse. Remember, he had played his high school and college ball in his hometown of Chicago, too—one of few who ever played high school, college and pro basketball in the same city. "Sitting on the bench in front of your home crowd…I felt like hiding," he said. "It was very difficult, a very difficult year."

He did play in 31 games, averaging 12.3 minutes, 5.5 points, 1.8 assists and 1.2 rebounds. He shot .706 from the foul line and a poor .333 from the field. But he did have moments to remember, good and bad.

When the Lakers, led by Elgin Baylor, came to Chicago for an exhibition game, it was played at DePaul's Alumni Hall. Possibly to hype the gate, Hershey got his one and only NBA start. He responded by scoring 22 points. "It was the only time he started and the only time he was given a real chance to play," Ira Berkow said.

Hershey will remember personal encounters with three NBA Hall of Famers.

In an exhibition game against Boston, he had the ball on a Packers' fast break. "I stopped at the foul line," Hershey said. "Bill Russell was under the basket, maybe eight feet from me. I shot a jumper and he blocked it. He took like half a step or a step, and blocked it. I still don't know how he did it." Russell did that to dozens of players.

Another Celtics great, Bob Cousy, also treated Hershey rudely. "They were beating us," Hershey said. "I got into the game and the first thing Cousy did was he went down in the pivot. Everybody thinks of him being small. He was 6-1. He towered over me. He took a hook shot and bounced it in over me. I felt embarrassed. I was out of the game in another two minutes."

However, Hershey has this sweet memory from a fast break against Wilt and the Philadelphia 76ers. Learning his lesson from Russell's block, he faked a pass, waited for Wilt to extend his arms and then drove underneath him to make a layup. "He was like a mountain," Hershey said.

There weren't many other highlights in Hershey's season. "It was frustrating for him," Ray Meyer said. "It was frustrating for me, too. I thought he could play."

Hershey (back row, third from left) with the Chicago Packers during the 1961-62 season.
Courtesy of Howie Carl

He never got a second chance. He was cut the following season as the Packers renamed themselves the Zephyrs. The next season they left Chicago and became the second version of the Baltimore Bullets before moving on to Washington, D.C.

Hershey went on with his life. He taught high school phys ed for two years and worked for State Farm as an insurance adjuster for one. He and Sam then opened a finance company. Hershey spent two years doing that, then moved on to become a trader at the Chicago Mercantile Exchange. He was there for 25 years, and recently retired. He and his wife Judy have three children, a daughter Cheryl, and two sons, Adam and Josh. Adam, who is 5-11 and 23 years old, went to Bradley University and transferred to Wisconsin, where he played one season of basketball. Josh, who's 5-8, played basketball in high school and is a non-playing freshman at Indiana University.

Thirty-four years later and counting, Hershey Carl is still all over DePaul's record book: first in career free throw percentage (.853), second (20.0) in career scoring average to NBA star Mark Aguirre (24.5), fifth in career free throws (425), and ninth in points (1,461).

He was surprised to learn only nine other players under 5-foot-10 have ever played in the NBA, and he was shocked when he heard that he was the tallest of the group: "I'm the tallest? First time in my life I was ever the tallest."

Statistics

Hershey Carl

Collegiate

Season	Team	G	Avg Pts	Avg Reb	FG Pct	FT Pct
1958-59	DePaul	24	19.2	4.5	.390	.826
'59-60	DePaul	24	19.7	4.6	.386	.864
'60-61	DePaul	25	16.3	3.5	.410	.875

NBA

Season	Team	G	Avg Pts	Avg Ast	Avg Reb	FG Pxr	FT Pct
1961-62	Chicago	31	5.5	1.8	1.3	.333	.706

They Played in the NBA at 5-foot-10

Ralph Beard ★★★★★★★★★★★★★★★★★★★★★★★★ Indiana

Jimmy Darrow ★★★★★★★★★★★★★★★★★★★★★ St. Louis

Sonny Herzberg ★★★★★★★★★★★★★★★★★★★★ Boston

Red Holzman ★★★★★★★★★★★★ Rochester/Milwaukee

"Fast Eddie" Hughes ★★★★★★★★★★★★★★ Utah/Denver

Avery Johnson ★★★★★★★★★★★★★★ Seattle/Denver/San
Antonio/Houston/Golden State

Slater "Dugie" Martin ★★ Minnesota/New York/St. Louis

Paul "Bucky" McConnell ★★★★★★★★★★★★ Milwaukee

Bob Royer ★★★★★★★★★★★★★★★★★★★★★★★★★★ Denver

Jerry Rullo ★★★★★★★★★★★★★★★★★★★★★★★ Philadelphia

Kenny Sailors ★★★★★★★★★★ Denver/Boston/Baltimore

Zeke Sinicola ★★★★★★★★★★★★★★★★★★ Fort Wayne

Willie Somerset ★★★★★★★★★★★★★★★★★★★ Baltimore

Index

I